The Clay Target Handbook

The Clay Target Handbook

A Manual of Instruction for all the Clay Target Shooting Sports

Jerry Meyer

Lyons & Burford, Publishers

This book is dedicated to Gil Ash—
a world class shooter, instructor,
photographer, friend, and perpetual
student of shotgun performance.

Design by M.R.P. Design

Printed in the United States of America
10 9 8 7 6 5 4 3 2 1

Library of Congress Cataloging-in-Publication Data

Meyer, Jerry, 1939–
    The clay target handbook : a manual of instruction for all the clay target shooting
sports / by Jerry Meyer.
        p.   cm.
    Includes index.
    ISBN 1-55821-176-4
    1. Trapshooting.   I. Title
GV1181.M43   1993
799.3'13—dc20   92-42628
                                                                                      CIP

Contents

Acknowledgments

The following individuals, gun clubs and manufacturers have all been major contributors to the completion of this book. In addition to providing assistance to me and this work, they are also major contributors to the clay target shooting sports and they deserve your appreciation and support.

These folks were extremely helpful during the year and a half it took to write this book. In the years prior to this project they have served well as coaches, instructors, shooting buddies, and, most importantly, as friends:

Gil Ash	Eric Beckman	
Dan Mitchell	Ed Scherer	E. L. Wilkins
Phil Murray	Sandy Wood	Jon Kruger
Burl Branham	Ken Davies	King Howington
Michael Murphy	Dan Carlisle	Kuo Cheng Ma
Jess Briley	Dan Schindler	Mike Hampton
Bud Decot	Roger Mitchell	Kay Arrington
Henry Burns	Marty Fischer	Lois Lessing
Del Hill	Jose Morales	David Fischer
George Bednar	Keith Lupton	Holly Haggard
John Horan-Kates	John Higgins	Jon Roosenburg

These clubs provided valuable assistance in photography and the use of facilities for field testing, research, and, most importantly, some great clay target shooting experiences over the years:

Wolf Creek Gun Club
Vail Rod & Gun Club
Sandanona Shooting School
Cherokee Rose Sporting Club
Hunters Ridge Sporting Clays
National Gun Club
Postl's Point Gun Club
Pigeon Mountain Sporting Clays
Southern Skeet & Trap Club
Shaw Rod & Gun Club

Selwood Hunting Preserve
Callaway Gardens Gun Club
Black Canyon Gun Club
Minnesota Horse And Hunt Club
Millrock Gun Club
Tyndal Air Force Base Gun Club
Shoot Fire Sporting Clays
Forest City Gun Club
Jefferson Gun Club
Montlake Shooting Center

The following shooting organizations provided statistics and technical advice:

National Rifle Association

National Shooting Sports Foundation

Amateur Trap Shooting Association

U.S. Army Marksmanship Unit

National Sporting Clays Association

National Skeet Shooting Association

These manufacturers provided products for testing and technical advice:

Beretta U.S.A.
Briley
Winchester
Remington
Federal Cartridge
Bob Allen

10-X
Rhino Manufacturing
Lincoln Traps
Holland & Holland
Windjammer
Mec Reloaders

Introduction

The research and writing of this book has taken over a year and a half. I have attempted to provide information on how to shoot the various clay target games for those who are interested in getting started or improving their shooting skill. As a shooting instructor, I have no illusions that this or any other book or videotape will teach you how to shoot. You will have to learn how to shoot. All I can do is give you some tools; you will have to make yourself into a mechanic.

It doesn't matter what your age is, your income, or physical ability. There is a clay shooting sport that you can shoot and shoot well. I have seen people in wheelchairs or so physically impaired that they could only hold their guns with one hand, but they enjoyed the satisfaction of turning a target to smoke or shooting a new personal best score. Everyone cannot be the world champion in a clay target sport. Only one person can do that. But everyone can attain their own peak performance and attain their goals of tournament winner, better wingshooter or just simply meeting new friends who also love shotguns. You don't have to win the Masters to enjoy golf or be a champion at Wimbledon to enjoy tennis.

Shooting clay targets creates a never ending season for the
shotgunner—no closed seasons, no limit, and nothing to clean
except your gun at the end of the day. Why leave your gun cased up
nine months of the year when you could be shooting year-round like
these guys at the American Shooting Centers in Houston, Texas?
Photo: Gil Ash

Clay target shooting can be anything you want it to be. Clay
shooting can provide a never-ending season for those hunters
who love shotguns and shooting them. Sporting clays can be an
educational opportunity to hone wingshooting skills in the off
season. For those who have never competed in sports, it provides
an opportunity to start a collection of trophies and medals.

Competing in your favorite clay target game at a local or
major tournament sure beats lying on the sofa and watching
others enjoy the thrill of victory and the agony of defeat. If you
want to compete in Grand American Trap Shoot or the World
Skeet Shooting Championship or the National Sporting Clays
Championship all you have to do is enter and go.

Your idea of shotgun fun may simply be a weekly visit to your
local gun club to shoot some clays with your buddies. You are not
alone, because this is the type of clay target shooting that is
enjoyed by more shooters than any other type.

If you really want to improve your shooting skills I suggest you arrange to attend a clinic or visit a club that offers shooting instruction. I also recommend that you join one of the associations that governs and promotes the particular version of clay target shooting you enjoy. All these groups have official publications that list clubs, tournaments, certified instructors, and information on how to shoot clay targets. I also suggest that you join the National Rifle Association, since it protects the rights of all of us to own and shoot firearms.

I hope that this book will give you enough information to get started in clay target shooting and trigger your career in a sport that has some of the nicest people you will ever meet as participants.

Between writing this book and teaching clinics I haven't had much time for shooting clay targets during the past year and a half. I intend to do some catching up real fast and see just how many empty hulls I can produce and maybe break a few targets along the way.

—JERRY MEYER
Talking Rock, Georgia

Basic Shotgunning

There are certain common elements that are conducive to acquiring basic shotgun shooting skills. Even though the various forms of clay target shooting vary in specific technique, format, and technology, the basics must be addressed to achieve anything near optimum performance. A partial list of those components includes:

GUN FIT

GUN MOUNT

TARGET BREAK POINT

EYE FOCAL POINT

GUN HOLD POINT

FORWARD ALLOWANCE

CHOKES AND LOADS

Each of these components will be addressed specifically and in detail as they relate to the individual clay target games in the following chapters. However, to prevent repetition, I want to emphasize their importance in obtaining optimum performance in all the clay target shooting sports.

The gun is correctly stocked to fit this United States Army Marksmanship Unit for International trap. A correct gun fit is critical to achieving optimal personal performance in your chosen clay target shooting sport.

Gun Fit—Why It Is Important

After many years as a clay target shooter and instructor, I am convinced that this is the most neglected component of good shotgunning skill. Shooters will spend hundreds or even thousands of dollars on guns, ammo, practice, and lessons and never even consider if their gun fits them. You can shoot a gun that doesn't fit you correctly. You may even shoot that ill-fitted scattergun quite well. But you will never shoot that gun up to your optimum potential if it doesn't fit you correctly.

The two most important elements in shotgunning are gun mount and gun fit. To break targets consistently the gun must be mounted precisely on each shot. Once you have mastered the subtleties of gun mount, the gun must shoot where you look.

There are some other factors that contribute to good shotgunning skills, but they are insignificant when compared to these two.

In America shotguns are stocked to fit the following "average shooter" who:

weighs 160 pounds;

is 5' 10" tall;

has a slender face with average cheekbones;

and has a 32" sleeve length.

The "average stock dimensions" to fit this "average shooter" are:

1½-inch drop at comb;

2½-inch drop at heel;

14-inch length of pull;

0 cast; and a

2-inch pitch.

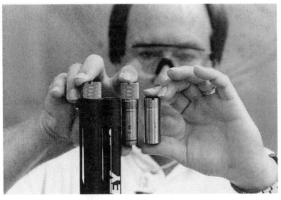

You owe it to yourself to get the best equipment you can afford. Experiment and test patterns to see which chokes and loads perform best in your gun for the various situations you may encounter in your particular clay target shooting sport. *Photo:* **Gil Ash**

According to gun fitter Michael Murphy, the above anatomical and gun measurements fit only about 10 percent of the shooters. Another 30–40 percent of the shooting population, which is fairly close to the average, can shoot a gun with these dimensions reasonably well. The further the remaining 50–60 percent deviates from the hypothetical "average" shooter, the more difficult it will be for it to shoot the standard factory-stocked shotguns.

Even if you are one of those shooters who meet the 5'10" height and 160-pound weight requirements, you might have other physical characteristics that would cause you to have difficulty shooting a factory-stocked gun. For example, a person of "average" height and weight might have wide cheekbones, close or wide-set eyes, a short neck, a long neck, wide shoulders or narrow shoulders.

How would you feel about buying suits, hats or shoes that only came in one size? I can see me trying to force my 6'1", 235 pounds, size 11 shoe and 7¾ hat size into an outfit made for a guy 5'10" and weighing 160 pounds. We insist that a seventy-dollar pair of shoes fit our specific size, but pay several thousand bucks for a shotgun and take any size we get.

A few definitions of gun stock fit and terminology are in order since they will be appearing in future chapters. The basic measurements are:

- *Length of pull* measured from the trigger to the center of the butt. If the gun has two triggers, the measurement is taken from the front trigger. The length of pull is usually pretty close to right if your nose is about 1½ inches from your thumb when the gun is mounted.

- *Drop at comb* determines the height of your eye over the barrels. Adjustments can be made by bending the stock up or down, adding or removing wood from the comb, or having your stock customized with an adjustable comb.

- *Cast-on* or *cast-off* is obtained by moving the butt to the right or the left of a straight line projected rearward from the barrels. Cast-on is achieved by moving the butt to the left of a straight line projected rearward from the barrels. Cast-off is obtained by moving the butt to the right of a straight line projected rearward from the barrels. Most mass-produced shotguns have very little cast. Some are slightly cast-off to accommodate right-handed shooters. This makes sense, since 85 percent of all shooters are right-handed. Unless, of course, you are left-handed; then it makes absolutely no sense at all!

- *Pitch* is basically the angle of the stock butt and can be altered by shortening the stock at toe or heel. This modification is most frequently done by shortening the distance to toe, reducing discomfort to female shooters.

- *Diameter of grip* Your thumb should touch your index finger when holding the grip.

- *Cast at toe.* The toe of a stock can be twisted left or right as an alternative to adjusting pitch by cutting wood off the stock at the butt.

There are several reasons why we American shooters accept ill-fitting scatterguns. The gun manufacturers don't offer a lot of choice. Shooters in this country have not demanded that a gun fit them. There are very few qualified gun fitters. There are a limited number of qualified stock makers who can produce a custom stock. Gun fitting and custom stock making can be expensive.

Many shooters who flinch, endure soreness in the face and shoulder, and suffer other unpleasant side effects of recoil do so quite frequently as a result of poor gun fit. A gun stocked too high will pound you on the cheekbone every time you shoot it. A gun stock with too much drop can cause excessive muzzle rise on each shot.

I must confess that after three decades of being a serious

This point-of-impact test, using a piece of bed sheet, indicates that the shooter's gun is slightly high and to the left.

upland gunner, I never worried or even thought about stock fit. Every time I bought a new or used gun, I snapped it to my shoulder a few times, aimed (yes aimed, because I didn't know any better) down the barrel and proclaimed it fit just right. Any shotgun will fit if you jam it into your shoulder and then move your head around until you align the bead with some stationary target on a gun shop wall. Even after getting hooked on target shooting and becoming fairly serious about it, I still didn't concern myself too much with stock fit.

Like most shooters who have only been able to afford factory-stocked guns, I learned to shoot guns stocked for the average shooter fairly well. I adapted myself to the gun rather than having the gun modified to fit me.

There are several fairly simple ways to test your gun for the correct fit. One that is fairly accurate can be done in your home with an empty gun. After checking to see that the gun is empty (something you should do each and every time you pick up a gun) locate an object such as a light bulb, or other feature on the wall. With a dismounted gun, focus your eyes on the object, close your eyes, mount the gun, then open your eyes. If the gun is not pointing at the target, then your gun doesn't fit or you mounted it incorrectly. If the gun is consistently pointing at the object after several of these drills then your gun and technique are correct.

I am seeing an increase in the concern for stock fitting and an increase in the number of qualified stock fitters in this country. I hope it is a trend that will continue. As of this writing I am scheduled to spend two weeks in Vail, Colorado, serving as an instructor in the Holland & Holland-sponsored shooting schools. I have a try gun ordered, which I will take with me to learn all the fine points of gun fitting from some of the Holland & Holland instructors, who are among the best gun fitters in the world. Afterward, I will include gun fits as an option at my shooting clinics.

To obtain an accurate gun fit requires a qualified gun fitter and a try gun. Many shade-tree gun fitters will tell you that you can determine stock fit by holding the grip and placing the butt in the bend of your elbow. If you can still reach the trigger, then they will proclaim that the gun fits. All this proves is that you have an elbow and a shotgun!

Once a competent gun fitter has obtained the correct measurements, then your gun can be modified by a stock maker to your specifications and your chances for optimum personal performance will soar.

Stocks may be modified by bending, removing wood, making an adjustable stock, or having a new custom stock made for you.

Gun Mount

One of the most repeated comments I hear from my British colleagues is that more targets are missed due to poor gun mount than having the incorrect forward allowance. The longer I teach shooting clinics the more I believe they are right.

To expect any modicum of consistency with the shotgun, the gun must be mounted correctly each and every time. I will be the first to admit that I have broken targets when the gun was incor-

It doesn't matter which clay target sport you participate in; gun mounts must be correct and consistent.

rectly mounted. In spite of your best efforts, you will occasionally get a mount that is bad and a target that still breaks. More times than not, a poor gun mount results in a shot gone awry, a target missed, and a trophy lost.

Irregular and unorthodox gun mounts detract from consistent eye-hand coordination. Excessive recoil punishment can also be expected if the stock is not placed in the correct position on your shoulder. Most reputable gun fitters won't measure you for a stock until you have shot long enough to develop your own personal style. Until you have the gun mount perfected and perform it consistently it is impossible to be fitted, since you will be mounting the gun in a different place on each shot.

Target Break Point

Shooting style and technique in all the clay target shooting games begins with where you expect to break the targets. In the disciplines of skeet and sporting clays you can determine almost exactly where you should break the target. In trap shooting, you can only determine an approximate zone where you can expect the target to be broken. The zone in international trap is considerably larger than the zone in American trap.

In all clay target sports, the target break point determines foot position, stance, gun hold point, eye focal point, type of forward allowance, choke, and load. In spite of its importance, I see many shooters who never give any consideration to where they will break the target.

Eye Focal Point

Almost as important as where you intend to break your targets is where you will look for them. This is another important aspect of clay target shooting that I see beginners completely disregard. Oh, they look for the target, but it is almost always in a different or incorrect location. Where the eyes are aimed and how they are focused often determine the degree of difficulty you will encounter on a target. Incorrect eye focal points can even eliminate any reasonable chance of breaking many targets.

The trap shooter who looks at his barrel as he calls for a target, the skeet shooter who looks for targets near the crossing stake, and the sporting clays shooter who looks where he expects to break the target are all making their respective sports more difficult than they should be.

It is best to shoot with both eyes open. If you shoot with only one eye open, you will lose half your peripheral vision and all of your three-dimensional depth perception. If you shoot with both eyes open, the dominant eye (also called the master eye) will take charge and direct the gun where it needs to go. You don't have to shoot with both eyes open. Some very good competitors shoot with only one eye open. But you will learn faster and shoot better if you learn to shoot with both eyes open.

To shoot with both eyes open, your dominant eye must be on the same side of the body that you shoulder the gun. Right-hand shooters must be right-eye dominant and lefties must be left-eye dominant. The test for dominant eye is simple. Tear a hole in the center of a sheet of typing paper, about the size of a dime. Holding one edge of the paper in each hand, straighten your arms out toward the ground. With both eyes open, focus on some object such as pine cone in a tree or the insulator on an electrical power pole. Keeping both eyes open, quickly raise the paper and center the object in the hole. Close one eye. If the object is still aligned in the hole, that is your dominant eye. If the object is not aligned, the other eye is dominant.

I suggest you read the excellent book on the role of vision in sports, *An Insight To Sports* by Dr. Wayne Martin. This book will absolutely improve your visual skills.

Gun Hold Point

Where you point your barrel can have a positive influence upon the difficulty of breaking any target. The right gun hold point can transform sheer panic into a target flying right into your waiting trap. A swing-through shooter and a sustained-lead shooter would have drastically different hold points on the same target. The swing-through shooter would have to hold his barrel closer to the trap machine for the target to pass by his muzzle early in its flight to allow him to come from behind and pass through the target at the optimum moment. To be caught behind a target is sure failure for the shooter who needs to see a sustained lead.

Shooters in my sporting clays clinics are amazed at how well a swing-through lead works when they learn the right combination of target break point, eye focal point, and gun hold point. If the gun hold point is wrong, neither swing-through nor sustained-lead will work and the shooter, whether realized or not, is reduced to the highly risky, low-success snap shot.

Most problems in all clay target shooting sports are usually directly related to gun hold points and it is one of the least understood and practiced skills. I am amazed at how many shooters concentrate on leads and never even consider gun hold points. They stand in utter amazement when they were sure they saw the correct lead, but the target flew on unscathed. The lead probably was good, but target break point, eye focal point, or gun hold point were either ignored or incorrect.

I have spent a great deal of time and money taking lessons from some of the best shooting instructors in the world and I never had a one of them address lead without including all the components that make any lead work, namely, target break point, eye focal point, and gun hold point. All are indispensable components of the equation that results in broken targets.

If you read this book from start to finish, you will get tired of seeing the following phrase: "Hold the muzzles just below the target flight line." That is because I see so many students poke their muzzles right up on the target flight line and the target either goes under the barrels completely or simply goes out of sight as it appears to fly into the sides of their barrels. Write this on your bathroom mirror, Chapter 12, Verse 6, Gospel according to St. Jerry: "THOU SHALT NOT EVER LET THE TARGET PASS BELOW THY BARRELS"

Forward Allowance

To put forward allowance into perspective, I want to share a little anecdote with you. I was on a dove shoot and it was one of those rare days when everything was working perfectly and I couldn't seem to miss. A very frustrated young man on the stand next to me, who was missing everything that flew over, could stand it no longer and swallowed his pride and walked over to me. "How far are you leading those birds?" he asked, expecting me to share some magical secret. I responded to his question with another question. "How long is a piece of string?" After letting him stand there for a few moments with a puzzled look on his face, I suggested he pretend that his gun was a paint brush. "Let the bird fly past your paint brush and then paint over him with one smooth stroke. Just as the brush passes over him, pull the trigger." He went back to his stand and immediately began dropping birds. I had told him how to use a swing-through lead. I wish I had learned his name, because he was undoubtedly one of the most teachable students I ever had.

This simple statement is the essence of using the swing-through method to obtain the forward allowance necessary to break a moving target. Let the target pass your barrels, swing the muzzles along the path of the target, and as you pass the target, pull the trigger. It is that simple and, simultaneously, that complicated.

For those of you with analytical minds, I will explain why this works. To overtake a target that has passed your barrels you must obviously be swinging faster than the target to catch it. If you pull the trigger as you pass it, your barrels will be out in front of the target when the shot load leaves the barrels. The faster the target is traveling, the faster you will have to swing to catch it, putting your muzzles farther in front by the time the shot exits the barrel.

The British have a term that explains why this lead works. They call it "sportsman's time." This is the time that elapses from the moment you decide to pull the trigger until the shot actually leaves the barrel. This includes your personal reaction time, from the time you decide to pull the trigger until the message reaches your trigger finger. After the trigger is pulled, several mechanical functions must occur. The trigger releases the sear, which allows the hammer to fall, striking the firing pin, which moves forward to dent the primer, which ignites the priming compound, which then ignites the powder charge that must burn, creating hot expanding gases that then push the shot charge down the barrel and out the muzzle. If you keep those muzzles moving you can create all the forward allowance you need while all this is taking place.

You cannot measure a lead or be deliberate in your actions when employing the swing-through method. This, more than any other method of obtaining forward allowance, depends on natural eye-hand coordination. There is not time to judge, measure, analyze, and calculate. The swing must be smooth, consistent, and positive. Any deliberation will bring unhappy consequences.

Swing-through lead is just one method of forward allowance. In a sporting clays clinic, I teach swing-through almost exclusively with only two variations for long, crossing shots. In a skeet clinic, I teach almost entirely sustained lead. International trap is a game of swing-through, forward allowance. American trap is a swing-through game, even though shooters with a high-combed, high-shooting trap gun see some daylight as they "float" the target above the barrels.

Sustained lead requires you to keep your barrels out in front of a target and pull the trigger when the appropriate space is seen between the barrels and the target. This gap and the barrels themselves are seen in the shooter's peripheral vision, with the eyes focused 100 percent on the target. The most difficult part of teaching someone to shoot with a sustained lead is to get them to avoid flicking their eyes back and forth from the barrels to the target. Another major problem is to get a student to avoid the temptation of looking back to the barrels just as the trigger is pulled to make sure the lead is right. Look at the target; just be aware that the correct lead is there.

The last and least desirable method of obtaining forward allowance is spot shooting, or snap shot, as some people call it. This method consists of picking out some patch of space toward which the target is flying and shooting at it, hoping that the shot swarm and target will occupy the same space at the same time. This is a last-ditch, panic-generated option that is rarely successful. Experienced shooters use it only as a last resort when they have been suckered by a Linda Ronstadt target—"Blue Bayou!"

Chokes and Loads

To make sure there is no misunderstanding about chokes and loads—you will not know exactly what a specific choke and load combination will do in your gun until you pattern it. Accept all advice and suggestions concerning chokes and loads as having a high probability of accuracy, but not as absolutes.

Many things affect pattern performance. The most significant is choke constriction. Choke constriction is measured and defined in several ways. You may have a trap gun with "modified" marked on the barrel. What does that mean? If you believe what you read and hear, modified choke means your barrel will place

The author uses this Beretta 682 sporting with 30″ barrels to shoot all clay target games including trap, skeet, sporting clays, International skeet and trap, and 5-stand sporting. This gun has also taken pheasants, ducks, doves, quail, chukars, grouse, and geese simply by changing chokes and loads. The availability of custom-after-market products (e.g. interchangeable screw in chokes and skeet tube inserts) allows maximum versatility in a modern over-and-under shotgun.

Typical Percentages of Pellets in 30-Inch Circle at 40 Yards	
CYLINDER	40
IMPROVED CYLINDER	50
MODIFIED	55
IMPROVED MODIFIED	65–75
FULL	70

55 percent of the shot in a 30-inch circle at 40 yards. You may also read or hear that modified choke is .010 to .020 constrictions. Still another source identifies modified choke as 18 to 22 points of constriction. To complicate matters even further, all or none of the above may be true for your specific gun!

A point of constriction is equal to one thousandth of an inch (.001). The standard by which chokes such as cylinder, skeet, improved cylinder, modified, improved modified, and full are determined is based on percentage of shot in a 30-inch circle at 40 yards.

I have a set of custom chokes made for me by Jess Briley that has the following constrictions:

Constriction in Thousands of an Inch	
.000	TRUE CYLINDER
.005	SKEET
.010	IMPROVED CYLINDER
.015	LIGHT MODIFIED
.020	MODIFIED
.025	IMPROVED MODIFIED
.030	LIGHT FULL
.035	FULL
.040	EXTRA FULL

The nomenclature for the chokes above are *not* based on the percentage of shot in a 30-inch circle at 40 yards, they are based on the points of constriction. This system simply uses the difference between the barrel diameter and the choke constriction as a means of labeling performance. You will notice a uniform difference of five thousandths of an inch (.005) in each choke, which is as small a differential as practical for most clay target applications.

The British have yet another system for designating choke:

British Choke System

FULL CHOKE	.040 CONSTRICTION
3/4 CHOKE	.030 CONSTRICTION
1/2 CHOKE	.020 CONSTRICTION
1/4 CHOKE	.010 CONSTRICTION
CYLINDER	.000 CONSTRICTION

I hope by now you understand why I said choke is a relative term. The only way to know what your gun produces with a specific choke and load combination is to test a few patterns. I think you will find it worth your time.

Many factors influence pattern performance—that is what all this business of choke and load is all about. It doesn't matter what is stamped on your barrel; what matters is the performance of your choke and load at the distance you will be shooting clay targets. Some trap shooters will swear modified choke is all you need for 16-yard singles. Another trap shooter will swear full choke is mandatory for 16-yard singles. They are probably shooting these targets from about 35 yards. And both of them could be right.

When a gun is mass produced the manufacturer has certain acceptable tolerances. Since these are tightly held secrets, you will never see these numbers in print. I suspect, based on using a bore micrometer on many shotguns in my clinics, that this is somewhere around plus or minus three thousandths of an inch. If those same tolerances are applicable to choke tubes, the same manufacturer could produce a gun with an actual bore diameter .003 under the standard of .729 and a modified choke .003 over .022, and you would have a whole choke size difference than a gun with a barrel of .003 over .729 and a choke tube .003 under .022.

Before you throw your gun in the trash, let me say that these are perfectly acceptable tolerances and that .001 of an inch is about the thickness of a cellophane wrapper off a pack of cigarettes!

Now throw into this equation other factors that affect pattern performance and tend to produce wider or tighter patterns:

Tighter Patterns	*More Open Patterns*
hard shot	soft shot
lower velocity	higher velocity
efficient wad columns	inefficient wad columns
efficient shot protection cups	no shot protection cups
lower peak ignition pressures	higher peak ignition pressures
larger shot	smaller shot

Factors other than pattern diameter influence target breaking capability. Two factors that should be considered are pellet distribution and pellet energy. A load of number 9 shot will produce the largest patterns and consistent density, but won't break many targets from the 25-yard line in handicap trap where targets are being shot at a distance of 40 yards or more. You can get a big pattern and adequate pellet energy by shooting 7½s in a cylinder choke, but due to the lower pellet count in a 1⅛ ounce load of

7½s, your pattern will be so sparse your 7½s might not even touch a target inside your pattern.

What this all boils down to is something that I call optimum pattern performance, which requires three characteristics:

1. The pattern must be dense enough to reasonably assure that several pellets will hit the target.

2. The pellets that strike the target must have sufficient energy to break the target upon impact.

3. The maximum diameter pattern that will perform requirements one and two.

To determine the optimum pattern for your gun you will have to use the above criteria and shoot some pattern paper at the ranges you will be shooting clay targets. Most clay target shooters who complain about pattern testing as drudgery have never done enough of it to see how enlightening it can be.

If you have spent much time around clay target shooters you have probably heard the old stick-your-head-in-the-sand philosophy, "I don't want to know how my gun patterns. I am breaking targets with it, and if I discover that it is throwing lousy patterns I

Barrel porting reduces recoil and muzzle jump. Ported barrels are allowed in all clay target shooting sports except International trap competition.

Speed up pellet counting with a hand talley counter, available at office supply stores. Shoot a few pattern tests to be sure how your gun performs at various distances with a specific choke and load combination. *Photo:* Gil Ash

will lost confidence in my gun." Bullfeathers! I have heard this statement many times myself, but it never came from a AA shooter in any of the clay target shooting sports. You can bet the trap shooter standing back on the 27-yard line knows what the choke and load he is shooting will do.

For those of you who lack the curiosity or the determination, I will offer suggestions on chokes and loads in each chapter that deals with a specific game, but they are general suggestions, and optimum pattern performance in your gun may be a whole choke or shot size away. Whether you plan to test patterns in your gun or not the following information may be of interest.

Tip: Barrel Check

Before we leave the subject of chokes and loads, I want to suggest you look through your barrels before loading that first shell. An obstacle in your barrels could cause severe damage to your gun and to you. It doesn't take much time and it identifies you as a safe and knowledgeable shotgunner.

Tip: Shot

One major dilemma faced by clay target shooters today is the standards of shot hardness. The problem is that there are no standards. Ammunition manufacturers or companies that distribute bagged shot for reloaders can label shot anyway they choose. Generally, chilled shot is the softest and because it has very little, if any, antimony, it is cheaper. This shot is found in the shells sold in discount stores and often referred to as "promotional loads." The best and hardest shot is usually found in a manufacturer's target loads. The bagged shot sold to handloaders may be labeled magnum shot, high antimony shot, or just about anything else and could mean just about anything.

The bottom line is, harder shot is deformed less during the impact of powder ignition and its journey down the bore. Consequently, less disfigured hard shot tends to fly in a more uniform trajectory and therefore remain inside the pattern. Softer deformed shot tends to fly erratically and drift outside the pattern, where it is ineffective.

So it comes down to this: the harder the shot, the more uniform and tighter the patterns will be. Softer shot tends to open patterns up more quickly for close-range shots in skeet and sporting clays. Plated number 7½ shot is hard and favored by world-class international trap shooters for their second shot. I know some savvy skeet and sporting clays shooters who use reclaimed shot for the close shots.

Larger shot tends to produce smaller pattern diameters than small shot when fired through the same choke constrictions. Increases in velocity tend to open up patterns a little quicker.

Since shot load is determined by weight, a load of large-size shot will have fewer pellets in a 1⅛-ounce load than the smaller size 9 shot. The following chart will illustrate the approximate number of pellets in a given weight of lead shot. This pellet count

Approximate Pellet Counts in Specific Weights of Lead Shot

Weight in Ounces	No. 7 ¹/₂	No. 8	No. 8 ¹/₂	No. 9
¹/₂ oz.	175	205	242	292
³/₄ oz.	262	308	363	439
⁷/₈ oz.	306	359	425	512
1 oz.	350	410	485	585
1 ¹/₈ oz.	393	461	545	658

will be slightly higher in shot with a high antimony content since antimony is lighter than lead.

Handloading your own shells for practice and competition is an option you may want to consider. I could lie to you and say that handloading will save you money. Handloaded shells are cheaper than factory loaded shells, but you probably won't save any money. If you are like the rest of us who handload, you still spend as much money—you just get to shoot more for the same amount of money.

I consider an evening spent in my basement loading shells a welcome alternative to an evening in front of the TV. The time I spend cranking shells out of my reloading press is relaxing and helps me unwind after a day's work. I also find reloading satisfying since I tend to measure my wealth not in dollars, but in how many buckets I have full of shotgun shells.

I know only a few serious shotgun shooters who do not reload shells, at least for practice, and they tend to be extremely well off financially. Those of us who have to make payments on the car and mortgage each month consider reloads a way of life.

If you are a new clay target shooter, I suggest you get a few books on shotshell reloading and ask several experienced reloaders for some advice on getting set up.

Since I tend to dabble in all clay target games, I started out with a press for each gauge, 12, 20, 28, and .410. These were all single Mec 600 Jr stage presses that required me to move each shell through the various positions on the press. I am now phasing out these single-stage presses as my budget allows and replacing them with Mec 9000 progressive reloaders.

I would suggest a new reloader start out with a single-stage press to both master the fundamentals of shotshell reloading and to get some experience. I believe you will then do as I did and upgrade to a progressive reloader.

Tip: "Bloopers"

A blooper is a defective shell that makes a strange report when fired. Anytime a shell sounds in any way different, the barrels should be checked for a stuck wad before another shot is fired. I have seen targets broken on skeet fields by "bloopers" and the wad never left the barrels! If you are shooting on a squad with someone who fires a "blooper" and he attempts to shoot again without checking his barrels, suggest that he check them, because you may be hit by shrapnel generated by his exploding barrels.

2 ▼

Trap

The first mention of trap shooting as a sport is found in a circa 1793 English publication, *Sporting Magazine*. The practice of shooting live birds from traps was first introduced to the United States in 1831 by the Sportsman's Club of Cincinnati, Ohio. Targets replaced live birds at about the time of the Civil War. Early replacements included "metal" birds with rotary wings and feather-filled glass balls designed to replace a live bird. In the 1880s, clay targets similar to the ones used today were first developed.

The first Grand American Handicap was held in 1900 in Queens, Long Island, and was the beginning of what has become the nation's most renowned shooting tournament. In 1924, Vandalia, Ohio, became the permanent home of The Grand. In recent years 6,000 participants shoot at 4½ million clay targets in the ten-day tournament!

Trap is the most popular clay target shooting sport in America, with approximately 55,000 active shooters who shoot an estimated 82.5 million registered targets per year. I repeat, *82.5 million registered targets per year.*

Actually there is no such thing as doubles in trap. There are only two singles in the air at one time. That is how you must think about them and this how you must shoot them—one at a time.

National Shooting Sports Foundation research indicates that the average new shooter breaks thirteen out of twenty-five targets on the first try at trap shooting and gradually improves through the high teens into the low twenties. NSSF also estimates that the average registered trapshooter breaks twenty-one out of twenty-five targets. Shooting a perfect score of twenty-five straight is a reasonable goal for a new trap shooter in his first year.

Singles, also called the "16-yard event" for reasons that will soon become apparent, are shot from five positions, which are located 16 yards behind the trap house. Targets are thrown at varying angles within the range of 45 degrees left or right of a straight-away target thrown from the middle shooting position, also known as post 3. These shooting stations are sometimes referred to as "pegs," "posts," or "stations." Targets will travel a maximum of from 48 to 52 yards from the shooter. Most single targets are shot at when they are in the neighborhood of 33 to 36 yards from the shooter. A round consists of 25 targets, with five shots being fired from each of the five shooting positions. After firing five shots on a position, all shooters rotate from left to right. The shooter on position 5 turns to his right and walks behind the other shooters to position 1. It is considered impolite for a shooter to turn to his left when leaving position 5, because this could cause him to turn into the shooter advancing from position 4, resulting in the guns being bumped together. Bumping your gun against someone's $5,000 gold-inlaid trap gun is not a good way to win friends and influence people on the trap field. Obviously all these movements occur with all guns unloaded and actions open. The British call this game Down The Line, which is often shortened to DTL.

In the handicap event a shooter may be required to stand anywhere from 17 to 27 yards behind the trap house. The determination of exactly where the shooter will stand in this event is based on previous scores and wins at a particular yardage. The better you shoot, the farther back you are moved. To be a 27-yard-line shooter requires a lot of work and carries with it well-deserved recognition from other shooters. You may hear veteran trap shooters refer to the 27-yard line as "shooting from the fence" or "shooting from the back yard."

Doubles are also shot from the 16-yard line. As their name implies, two targets are launched simultaneously. One will be at about 35 degrees to the right of the imaginary line going straight-away from the middle position and the other target will travel at about a 35 degree angle to the left of straight-away. You are allowed only one shot at each target. A standard round of doubles is 25 pair or 50 targets.

Guns

The typical gun for trap shooting is a 12 gauge with full or improved-modified choke and a ventilated rib barrel 30–32 inches long. Although many top trap shooters favor over/under shotguns, single barrels, autoloaders, and even pumps are common. Most guns used exclusively for shooting American trap are stocked to shoot higher than field, skeet, or sporting clays guns.

Since American trap targets are always rising, a high-shooting gun allows the shooter to "float" the target above his barrels so he can see the target as it is shot. Registered trap is always shot with a 12 gauge.

Over-and-unders dominate the field in trap doubles. There are several reasons for this. The most overwhelming is the advantage of having two separate chokes, one for the closer-than-usual first target and one for the farther-than-usual second target. The top shooters tend to favor tight chokes in both barrels for those smoke balls that intimidate us garden-variety trap shooters. The great majority of trap shooters will benefit from having light modified or even a tight improved cylinder in that first barrel. Another advantage of a slightly open choke in the first barrel is that it affords a little more margin of error in pointing mistakes when taking that first target as fast as possible.

Don't feel like you have to go out and buy a custom trap gun to enjoy trap shooting and shoot good scores. If you have a 12 gauge shotgun choked modified or full, all you need is some eye and ear protection and you are ready to begin your career in trap shooting. I shoot trap with the same 682 Beretta Sporting Clays over-and-under, with 30-inch barrels, that I use for sporting clays, skeet, international trap, international skeet, and hunting. With the availability of interchangeable screw-in chokes, the same gun can be used for many different games. I also have several stocks for this gun so I can switch to one with less drop at comb to use for rising trap targets.

Chokes and Loads

There are a few rules of thumb you can apply in selecting chokes and loads for trap. One is that most shooters will shoot single and handicap targets 16–20 yards from the trap house. Add this distance to the distance of the shooter behind the trap house and

Shooters who occupy the 27-yard line in handicap events usually opt for full choke and a number 7¹/₂ shot. *Photo:* Jennifer Maier

you have a reasonable distance to pattern chokes and loads. As an example, if you are shooting singles from the 16-yard line, you will be shooting targets in the neighborhood of 33 to 36 yards. If you are a handicap shooter, shooting from the 27-yard line (27 yards behind the trap house), you will be shooting targets at distances of 43 to 47 yards.

In 16-yard singles and handicap back to about the 20-yard line, 2¾ dram or light loads of 1⅛ ounces of number 8 shot are probably the most common loads. Once shooters get behind the 20-yard line you begin to see the 3-dram loads with 1⅛ ounce of 7½s take over.

In doubles, the first target is shot at closer than 36 yards from the shooter and the second is shot farther than 36 yards from the shooter. Doubles are the only targets in trap launched at the same angles every time. In 16-yard singles and handicap, you never know if you are getting a straight-away, a left-hand crosser or right-hand crosser. In doubles, you know where they are coming from and where they are going so you can "ambush" that first target before it gets 36 yards away. Even with the advantage of the known trajectory and the chance to shoot the first target early, the second target will still have traveled more than 36 yards from the shooter before he takes the shot. Knowing this, it is reasonable to conclude that you can open up the choke a little on that first target to get a bigger pattern and tighten up on the second barrel and use 7½s to have the pattern density necessary to break the distant second target.

Tip: Harvesting Empties

Many trap shooters are reloaders. We come to the line with all sorts of bags and pouches to hold our treasured empties. In spite of your best efforts, you will occasionally drop an empty shell during the course of shooting a round. Leave it on the ground. It can be very distracting to your fellow shooters to have you step off the station to retrieve an empty. If you drop a live shell and need it to finish the round, wait until you have shot all your targets on that station and pick it up during the change. *It is a rule at many clubs that any empties that hit the ground belong to the club.* This is to prevent shooters from harvesting empties during a round. This is not only discourteous, it can be very dangerous. Be polite, be safe or be gone!

When leaving post 5 during the changing of posts, turn to your right and away from the shooter who is approaching you from post 4. This may not sound like a big deal, but it will be when you turn to your left and put a ding in some guy's trap gun that is covered with gold ducks!

As in all clay shooting sports, keep that action open except when on position and ready to call for a target. If you see someone walking around with his action closed, ask him to open it. Embarrassment is his friend—it helps him learn.

Trap Targets

Trap targets are 4⁵⁄₁₆ inches in diameter and 1⅛ inches in height, weighing 3½ ounces.

How To Shoot Trap

One of the often repeated phrases you hear around gun clubs is, "Skeet is hard to learn, but easy to shoot. Trap is easy to learn, but hard to shoot." If you consider that skeet shooters have to deal with eight stations, each of which has targets going in opposite directions and some with doubles, I would say, yes, skeet is harder for a new shooter to learn. A new trap shooter doesn't have all the technical detail to learn, but neither does he have those consistent targets and leads that can be fine-tuned on a target-by-target basis by a dedicated skeet student. The trap shooter has to learn how to read every target and make a split-second decision on what it takes to break that target. I contend that both games require a concentrated effort to attain your personal peak performance, and none of them is "easy" if you want to dedicate yourself to shooting consistently high scores and winning major tournaments.

Target Break Point

You never know exactly where a trap target will go. You do know that it will be somewhere within the prescribed boundaries. Therefore, you must position yourself to break a target anywhere within bounds. I will offer some specific suggestions as I address how to shoot each position. The great D. Lee Braun suggested that a trap shooter position his feet so that a line drawn across the toes of both feet would parallel the path of the extreme left-hand target. For left-handers it was just the opposite; a line across the toes paralleled the path of an extreme right-hand target. I first read this more than 20 years ago and I have not found a better way to describe foot position on the trap field.

Eye Focal Point

It is best to avoid looking over your barrels, if you are a two-eyed shooter, when calling for a target. If you don't see a target until it gets up around the level of your barrels, you will play the very devil breaking it before it leaves the county. Cut your eyes slightly down toward the top of the trap house. I don't suggest you look right at the edge of the trap house—look out slightly in front.

Shooters who use one eye will need to hold their barrels slightly below the front edge of the trap house roof and look down their barrels to enable them to see the target as soon as it emerges from the house.

Gun Hold Points

There are several theories on gun hold points for trap. Some people adhere to the philosophy that gun hold points should favor extreme left or right crossing targets. Others suggest that straight-aways are the most frequently missed targets and set up to favor them.

I suggest the following hold points for a two-eyed, right-handed shooter. On position 1, hold the barrels directly over the front left-hand corner of the trap house. On position 2, hold halfway between the left front corner of the trap house and the center of the trap house. On position 3, right-handers should hold slightly to the right of the center of the trap house. This slightly off-center hold allows you to see a true straight-away target quickly. If you got a true straight-away and were holding dead-center on the trap house it would be obscured by the barrels and you wouldn't see it until very late in its flight. On position 4, hold halfway between the center of the trap house and the right front corner. On position 5, hold directly over the right front corner of the trap house. Some right-handed shooters like to favor the extreme right-hand target by moving the gun hold points on both positions 4 and 5 a little more to the right of those suggested above.

The gun hold points for two-eyed shooters should be about 18 inches above the trap house. Have someone measure this with a yardstick so you can see what 18 inches looks like. If you don't have a yardstick, a stack of 40 targets is about 18 inches tall.

The gun hold points above are the same for a left-handed, two-eyed shooter expect for position 3. On position 3, the left-handed shooter should hold slightly to the left of the center of the front edge of the trap house roof.

One-eyed shooters cannot hold above the trap house roof line because their limited vision prevents them from seeing the target come out of the house. Consequently, they must lower their barrels to a position below the front edge of the trap house roof. On position 3 the hold point is dead center on the front edge of the trap house roof and slightly below it. It is not necessary to hold very far below the roof edge, just enough to prevent your barrels from blocking your view of the exiting target.

In my clinics I use stacks of targets to teach new shooters where to hold on the house at each position.

Holding the barrels horizontal is a good technique to determine how high to hold over the trap house before calling for a target. Some shooters may need to make slight adjustments but this is a good starting position for new inexperienced shooters, and for those who shoot with both eyes open. Shooters who shoot with one eye must point the barrels just below the front edge of the trap house so they can see the target as it emerges.

How high to hold over the trap house is probably one of the most discussed topics among trap shooters. Assuming you are a new shooter, I would suggest you begin by holding your barrels exactly horizontal. There might be some disagreement over just what one foot or eighteen inches over the trap house looks like from 16 yards away. Everyone can agree on what horizontal is. As you gain experience, you may want to raise or lower your barrels to fit your own style, but this will probably be pretty close to right.

Tip: Wind-Blown Trap Targets

If the wind is at your back it will force trap targets down. If a target gets below your barrels it can be very difficult to see and almost impossible to hit. Even if you see it you will have to be lowering your barrels while the target is rising. If the wind is blowing against your back, lower your hold point slightly. If the wind is gusting, you may have to use your regular hold point when it stops and lower it again if you feel wind as you call for the target. This low gun hold point may even have to be as low as the top of the trap house. As a rule I recommend a gun hold point much higher for two-eyed shooters.

As a general guide to the correct elevation for gun hold points for two-eyed shooters, the barrels are usually parallel to the ground for normal targets. For targets with tail winds blowing from behind your back, you may have to bring your barrels clear down to some point below the front edge of the trap house roof. For targets flying into a head wind, your hold point may need to be a high as 30 to 36 inches.

Only experience and shooting a lot of wind-blown targets will determine what is best for your specific style, but these suggestions will give you some parameters within which to work. I suggest you make an effort to schedule a practice session the next time your local weather forecaster predicts windy conditions.

Foot Position

Since you don't know exactly where your target will go, you do know that you will shoot it either as a straight-away or somewhere out to your left. When you are on position 1 and get a target that is launched to the extreme right of the trap house, it will be a straight-away. All other targets will be anywhere from slightly to your left or a good deal to your left. Therefore, your foot position should be such that you can swing easily anywhere the target goes. As a rule, most shooters tend to set their foot position to favor the extreme left-hand target.

Position One

On position 1, the gun hold point should be directly over the front left corner of the trap house and about 18 inches above the front edge of the trap house roof, if you are a two-eyed shooter. One-eyed shooters will need to align their barrels with the left

Gun hold point for post 1. Hold over the left front corner of the trap house. A two-eyed shooter holds on the top target in the stack, a one-eyed shooter holds on the bottom. The single target is to mark the center of the front edge of the trap house. I suggest that two-eyed shooters hold their barrels in a horizontal position for the best elevation. Personal shooting style or windy conditions may require slight adjustments up or down.

33
▼

Gun hold point for post 2. Halfway between the left front corner and the center of the front edge of the trap house. On post 1, the two-eyed shooter holds on the top target in the stack and the one-eyed shooter holds on the bottom target. To give you an idea of the stack height, it contains forty-six targets.

front corner of the trap house, but will need to lower their barrels below the front edge of the trap house roof to enable them to see the target come out of the house. A one-eyed shooter must keep his muzzle below the front edge of the roof on all positions to be able to see the target as quickly as possible.

Be sure your foot position will allow you to swing through on the extreme left-hand target on position 1. Left-handers may want to experiment with a gun hold point that is slightly to the left of the trap house corner.

Position Two

On position 2, the gun hold point should be about halfway between the left front corner and dead-center of the front edge of the trap house roof. I do not suggest you shift your foot position too much to the right on this station, especially if you are a left-handed shooter. Lefties may also want to try shifting the gun hold point a little toward the corner of the trap house.

Gun hold point for post 3 for right-handed two-eyed shooter. If you hold dead center on the trap house, you won't see a true straightaway target until it is a great distance from the house, so hold a little to the right of dead center on the house. A one-eyed shooter could hold dead center on the house to hold just below the edge of the trap house roof on all targets.

Position Three

Right-handers should hold 6–8 inches to the right of dead-center, left handers about the same distance to the left. One-eyed shooters need to be dead-center and just below the roof line. The most missed targets on this station are usually those that appear to be straight-away targets, but are actually very slight angles to either side of dead straight-away. You will usually know just after you pull the trigger that you read it wrong. This is a mental error rather than a technical one. Focus on the target and read it before you shoot. Don't rush this shot.

Position Four

The gun hold point here is halfway between the center of the front edge of the trap house and the right front corner. We are now moving into the stations where right-handers begin to have

trouble with the extreme right-hand targets. Some of this is anatomical. Right-handers swing better to the left, left-handers swing
better to the right. But it is mostly mental errors that cost you
targets on positions 4 and 5 when you get the right-hand crossing
targets. The tendency is to be intimidated and get deliberate. This
deliberation and trying to be sure interrupts your natural rhythm
and slows your swing. Be aggressive and shoot this target with
the same timing as the others. As I suggested for lefties on the
other side of the house, right-handers may want to move the gun
hold point slightly to the right.

Position Five

The best way to avoid losing targets on 5 is to be ready when you
call for the target. Don't let negative thoughts occupy your mind.
Look, really look, for every target when you call. On 5 you must
not only look, but react smoothly when you see it crossing to
your right.

**Gun hold point for post 3 for left-handed two-eyed shooter. A left-
handed shooter holds just to the left of center to avoid having the
barrels obscure the true straightaway target.**

Gun hold point for post 4. The gun hold point for post 4 is halfway between the center of the front edge and the right front corner of the trap house roof. Two-eyed shooters hold on the top target in the stack, while one-eyed shooters hold on the bottom target.

Gun hold point for post 5. The gun hold point is right over the front right-hand corner of the trap house roof. Two-eyed shooters hold on the top target in the stack, while one-eyed shooters hold on the bottom target.

Tip: Dealing With "No Target"

You will frequently see trap shooters get visibly upset with quick pulls, late pulls, and broken targets. These situations are outside the control of the shooter. Don't let them get blown out of proportion and cost you three or four targets because you lost your temper. My great-grandmother frequently used this advice when I was growing up and was prone to losing my temper when things didn't go exactly like I wanted them to, saying "If you come home and find someone has left a big bucket of wet cow manure in your living room, kicking it is not always the best solution." Take a deep breath, forget the quick pull or broken target. You can't shoot the trap boy or the last target, you can only shoot the next target. That, and only that, should occupy your thoughts and focus.

Trap Doubles

When shooting doubles, the eyes should flick directly to the second target as soon as the first one is broken. Direct the eyes to the second target immediately; the gun will follow. This principle applies to all the clay target shooting sports with double targets. *Photo:* Gil Ash

Tip: Eye Movement To Second Target

Any delay in shooting the second target welcomes disaster. One of the most important factors in breaking the second target in doubles is to see the second target as quickly as possible. To avoid delay, shift your eyes to the second target as your gun is recoiling from the first shot. Experienced shooters shift their eyes as they are pulling the trigger, but this takes a lot of practice. Understand that I am not suggesting you turn your head or take your cheek away from the stock. Only the eyes are shifted to the second target; the face stays on the stock and the gun is brought into alignment with the target by swinging the whole upper body.

Guns

The gun of choice for most doubles shooters is the over-and-under. There are several reasons for this choice. The over-and-under provides two choke choices. The first target must be taken quickly; therefore a more open choke producing a larger pattern is desirable. The second target in doubles requires a little more constriction. With a single-barrel autoloader allowing only one choke choice, you have to compromise on one of the targets in doubles.

It is desirable to shoot the first target quickly, recover as quickly as possible, and go to the second target without delay. When I have an experienced trap shooter who is having trouble with the second bird in doubles, the first two things I look at are how quick he takes the first target and how much time he loses going to the second target.

Always shoot your bottom barrel first when shooting any doubles, trap, skeet, or sporting clays. The bottom barrel has less muzzle jump than the top, allowing a quicker recovery. Jess Briley makes a device called the comp choke, which greatly reduces muzzle jump on the first shot in doubles. These are custom chokes that can have just the right amount of constriction for shooting the first shot in doubles. Porting your barrels will also reduce both muzzle jump and recoil on the first shot.

Some recoil-sensitive shooters use one-ounce loads on this first shot. If recoil bothers you, you might want to also consider several of the recoil-reducing devices advertised in *Trap And Field Magazine.*

Load choices for doubles depend on several factors. If you are shooting an autoloader with only one choke option, I would suggest 8s on the first shot and 7½s on the second. If you are shooting an over-and-under, I would recommend 8s in a tight improved cylinder or light modified choke and 8s in an improved modified or full for the second target. If you are taking both shots quickly as I recommend, then the more open chokes would be good choices. If you are getting to the second target a little late, you will need to consider tighter chokes and 7½s. Chokes and loads for doubles are difficult to be specific about since there is so much variation in how different individuals shoot these targets. I definitely recommend that you do some pattern testing at the ranges at which you shoot both the first and second targets.

If you do not choose to test your chokes and loads and want a simplistic answer, I recommend modified and full in an over-and-under.

Which Target First?

There are two schools of thought on which target should be taken first. Most everyone agrees that on positions 1, 2, and 3 the right-hand target should be taken first. These targets are either straight-aways or almost straight-aways. On positions 4 and 5, some shooters believe that it is better for right-handers to continue shooting the right-hand target first to allow unobstructed vision for picking up the second target. They feel that the barrels could obscure their vision when they shoot the left target first on positions 4 and 5.

On post 3 three doubles right handers should take the right-hand target first. Lefties should break the left-hand target first. This allows the shooter to maximize visibility of the second target.

Most of the top double shooters do not adhere to that theory and choose to shoot the left target first on 4 and 5 since they are the most straight-away targets and the easiest to shoot quickly. They also agree that it is difficult to shoot a hard-crossing right-hand target, stop your swing, and then come back to a target going almost straight away from you and avoid swinging to the left of the second target.

I suggest you shoot the left-hand targets first on 4 and 5. If you shoot them quick enough, your barrels should not obscure your vision when shifting your eyes back to the right for the second target, since they will still be fairly low. If the targets are rather low to begin with or are being held down by a tail wind, you can dip your barrels slightly as you swing back across the field for the second shot.

Tip: Take The First Target Quickly

It is important that you take the first target as quickly as possible. You must take chances on the first target because any deliberation or lost time on the first target greatly increases the degree of

On posts 4 and 5, most shooters have better luck taking the left target first because it is close to straightaway on 4 and *is* straightaway on 5.

When shooting doubles, take the first target as quickly as possible. This is not as risky as being slow on the first target and having to shoot the second as a long-dropping target.

difficulty on the second. Delay on the first target adds the complications of distance, wind, and a dropping target to the equation. Sure it is risky to take this first target quickly, but the risk is greater if you delay the second shot any longer than you absolutely have to.

Position One

On this position, shoot the right-hand target first and shoot it quick. Pick out some landscape feature to mark the target flight path. Your gun hold point should be directly on that flight path. Position your eyes so that you will see the target as it comes out of the house. Take a short stroke on the target and immediately shift your eyes to the left to see the other target. The gun will catch up with your eyes and when you see the correct lead, break it. I have seen all sorts of complicated charts on just how far to lead trap targets and find them to be confusing. The best system for learning the correct leads in trap is to shoot a lot of trap targets. Trap targets are all broken with the swing-through method.

Your foot position should favor the second shot since you will be performing a vigorous right-to-left swing when you take the second target to your left. Position your feet as though you were only shooting the second target. There is no swing required for the first target, just a short lifting stroke to the target.

As soon as the trigger is pulled, immediately shift your eyes to the second target. Keep your head on the stock.

Position Two

The procedure is the same as on position 1. Mark the target flight path with some landscape feature and place your gun hold point directly on the flight path of the target. Your eye focal point should be at the exact spot where the target comes out of the house. Shoot the first target as quickly as possible and immediately shift your eyes to the second target.

Position Three

On this position, the instructions change for the left-handed shooter. Left handers should shoot the left-hand target first to allow for increased peripheral vision on the second shot. Right-handers should take the right-hand target first for the same reason. Everything else is the same; mark the target flight path of the first target, focus your eyes on the spot where the target comes out of the house, break it quick, and shift the eyes immediately to the second target, and break it.

Position Four

Left-handers and right-handers are both back on the same sheet of music now as both take the left-hand target first. Remember: mark the flight path of the first target, break it quick, immediately shift your eyes to the second target and break it.

Position Five

The left target is broken first using the same system as on the other positions. A key factor to breaking the second target on both 5 and 1 is quick eye movement to the second target. It is always important to break the first target quickly and to shift your eyes to the second target. But since the second target on both 1 and 5 is so far away, quick eye movement is imperative.

Tip: Gun Hold Point—Key To the Quick Break

I have emphasized the importance of breaking the first target quickly. This shot is not made with a dead gun. There is a short swing involved in making this shot. You may need to experiment with the elevation of your gun hold point to determine what is best for your particular combination of visual ability and eye-hand coordination. If you seem to be waiting for the target after you see it come out of the house, lower your gun hold point. If it takes a long stroke or swing for you to catch the target, then raise your gun hold point slightly.

3

▼

American Skeet

Skeet was invented by an enterprising grouse hunter, Charles Davies, in Andover, Massachusetts, around 1920. Charley wanted to sharpen his wingshooting skills to improve his score on grouse.

The original layout was a complete circle not unlike the face of a clock, with a single trap located at 12 o'clock, which threw targets directly over 6 o'clock. A shooting station was located at each number on the clock face. The diameter of this original circle was about 50 yards. It isn't surprising that the original version of the game was called "shooting around the clock." As the story goes, one of Charley's neighbors built a chicken house near their property line, which eliminated half of the shooting stations. When faced with this dilemma, Charley cut the circle in half and came up with the basic half-circle still used today.

In the original version of this game, the rules included a 3-second delay and the shooter was required to have a dismounted gun when the target was launched. I find it rather ironic that this original version of skeet, with 3-second delay and dismounted gun, invented in America by Americans, is now known as International Skeet and we

Americans are shooting a game with no delay and a mounted gun.

The year 1926 saw what is considered the first national tournament and the first 100 straight, which was shot by H. M. Jackson of Garner, North Carolina. Later that year the National Skeet Shooting Association was formed, which with one reorganization became the current organization that sanctions the American version of the sport.

In the early days before automatic electric traps, trap boys operated hand-set traps in each house. Because it was sometimes difficult to understand which house the shooter was calling "pull" for, a system was devised whereby a shooter called "pull" for the high house and "mark" for the low house. You will still hear some veteran shooters call "mark" for a low-house target.

As this is being written near the end of 1991, the National Skeet Shooting Association has 18,000 members and 7,000 affiliated gun clubs, which held over 2,000 registered tournaments and threw somewhere between 18 and 19 million registered targets in 1991.

As impressive as those numbers are, there are many more shooters who still shoot skeet to hone wingshooting skills for hunting or as a casual recreational sport. National Shooting Sports Foundation research indicates that the average shooter breaks 11 targets out of 25 in his first try at skeet. To shoot registered targets you must be a member of the National Skeet Shooting Association. (See appendix for information.)

How the Game Is Shot

Skeet is shot in squads of five shooters or fewer. Before attempting his first target on station 1, the squad leader has the option of viewing a high single, a low single, and a pair of doubles. The high-house opening is 10 feet above the ground and the low-house opening is 3 feet above the ground.

**Both trap and skeet fields are wheel chair accessible.
Many of the major shoots have concurrent wheel chair
events.**

Guns are kept open and unloaded until the shooter is on
station and ready to shoot. Any conversation that would distract
the shooter should be avoided. Shooters should not advance to
the next station until the entire squad has finished shooting.

When shooting doubles, always shoot the outgoing target
first. New shooters tend to rush their shots when shooting
doubles.

One round of skeet consists of 25 shots fired from eight
different stations in the following manner:

- Station 1
  - –1 high-house single
  - –1 low-house single
  - –1 pair of doubles (shoot high house first)
- Station 2
  - –1 high-house single
  - –1 low-house single
  - –1 pair of doubles (shoot high house first)
- Station 3
  - –1 high-house single
  - –1 low-house single

- Station 4
  - −1 high-house single
  - −1 low-house single

- Station 5
  - −1 high-house single
  - −1 low-house single

- Station 6
  - −1 high-house single
  - −1 low-house single
  - −1 pair of doubles (shoot low house first)

- Station 7
  - −1 high-house single
  - −1 low-house single
  - −1 pair of doubles (shoot low house first)

- Station 8
  - −1 high-house single
  - −1 low-house single

The total of the above shots is 24. If the shooter has not missed a target, his 25th shot will be another station 8 low house. If he misses before that, he will repeat the first target he missed.

Registered skeet is shot with four gauges, 12, 20, 28, and .410. A major tournament usually consists of 100 targets in each gauge plus 100 doubles. The groupings are:

- 12-gauge event—open to 12-gauge guns or smaller.

- 20-gauge event—open to 20-gauge guns or smaller.

- 28-gauge event—open to 28-gauge guns or smaller.

- .410-bore event—open to .410-bore only.

Tip: Don't Mix Shells

Don't mix shells of different gauges in shooting vest pockets or shell bags. If a 20-gauge shell is inadvertently dropped into the chamber of a 12 gauge, the 20 will fall completely out of sight and lodge in the end of the chamber and the forcing cone. There will still be enough room in the chamber for a 12-gauge shell to enter the chamber behind the 20 gauge. When the gun is fired it will immediately be transformed into a pipe bomb. I have seen several guns that were blown up and was very surprised that both shooters survived.

Skeet Doubles

In tournaments, doubles events require a minimum of 50 targets. This is also the way doubles are usually shot just for fun in a more casual atmosphere.

Shooting commences at station 1 and continues over to station 7 (no doubles are shot on station 8), then continues back to stations 6, 5, 4, and 3, and ends after shooting station 2. When progressing from left to right around the field or from station 1 to station 7, the high-house target is shot first. When going in the opposite direction, from station 7 back toward station 1, the low-house target is shot first on station 4.

Doubles are also used to break ties in skeet tournaments. If at the end of the regular program two or more shooters are tied for an individual event or high overall, the tie is broken by shooting doubles at stations 3, 4, and 5. As in regular doubles, when moving from station 3 to 4 you shoot the high-house target first on station 4. When advancing from station 5 to station 4, you shoot the low-house target first on station 4.

Skeet Guns

For casual shooters, just about any scattergun with open chokes can be used for skeet shooting. In fact, a sizable portion of all skeet targets is broken by hunters who come to the local gun club to shoot a few clays prior to the opening of bird season.

More serious skeet shooters and tournament shooters will usually shoot either an autoloader or an over-and-under. Some use both. It is not at all unusual for a serious competitor to use a soft recoiling autoloader in the 12-gauge or doubles event, and a tubed over-and-under in the 20-gauge, 28-gauge, and .410-bore events.

I cannot recall anything except a tubed over-and-under winning one of the small-gauge events at the World Skeet Shoot or other major tournament in recent years. Tubed sets outnumber four-barrel sets considerably at the World Skeet Shooting Championships. At the 1990 World Shoot, 678 competitors opted for tube sets, with only 259 selecting four-barrel sets. In 1991, the spread was even greater, with 662 tube sets and only 140 four-barrel sets. There are numerous advantages to using a tubed over-and-under if you plan to shoot all four gauges in skeet.

One major advantage is economy. The cost of a top-grade tube set may sound expensive to the newcomer, but when com-

Tube sets manufactured to the exact dimensions of your gun barrels allow skeet shooters to use the same gun in 12, 20, 28, and .410 events by simply changing tubes. They are also available with interchangeable screw-in chokes.

pared to the cost of four skeet guns, they are a bargain. In addition to being economical, they contribute to higher scores. This is achieved in several ways.

When you use a tube set, you are looking over the same barrels and pulling the same trigger in all four gauges. When I first started shooting skeet I considered purchasing four Remington 1100s chambered for 12 gauge, 20 gauge, 28 gauge, and .410 bore. I changed my mind when I shot a few rounds with the .410 bore. That tiny little barrel intimidated me so much that I became very deliberate and tried to measure every shot, which resulted in a very poor performance. On the other hand, with a tubed 12 gauge over-and-under, I felt like I was shooting a "big" gun and swung with confidence. The added weight of a tube set, about 13 ounces, also contributes to a smooth swing and follow through, two vital components to stellar performance on a skeet field.

Barrel weights that weigh the same as your smaller-gauge tubes can be attached to your barrels when shooting the 12 gauge so the gun will balance and swing the same as when you are shooting smaller gauges with the tubes inserted.

When you send your over-and-under to have a tube set made, the manufacturer will measure your barrels and produce a tube for the top barrel and a tube ffor the bottom barrel. These tubes are not interchangeable between top and bottom or with any other gun!

Modern tubes have come a long way since Claude Purbaugh made the first sets in his California gunshop. Purbaugh's early tubes did not have integral extractors, so the tubes and extractors had to be changed between events. The Briley skeet tubes in my Beretta 682 even have interchangeable choke tubes for all gauges and straight rifling for more consistent patterns in the small gauges.

While not as common as they used to be, there are still a few four-barrel sets around. A four-barrel set consists of a single receiver with four sets of barrels in 12, 20, 28 and .410.

Some Basic Principles

Foot Position

Gil Ash, my teaching partner at many NSCA Instructor Certification Courses, has a little admonition that goes, "Feet and failure both begin with F." This little phrase is intended to impress upon our prospective instructors that the feet must be in the correct position to allow consistent swing and follow through. Misplaced feet can eliminate any possibility of hitting targets with any consistency. There are some who advocate moving the feet to different positions for singles and doubles on the same station. There are some shooters who make this changing of foot position work very well for them. I have seen some very good shooters using both methods.

Foot Position vs. Stance

Foot position and stance are two different functions. Foot position is *where* you stand, stance is *how* you stand. You will probably see

This photograph of Sid Dykes pivoting on his left leg illustrates the correct way to swing at a target. Swaying results in missed targets. Both his nose and front knee are directly over the toes of his front foot which contributes to a good pivot as opposed to an undesirable sway.

more variations in stance than in foot position among top shoot-ers. The really good, consistently top shooters are almost boring to watch. They lock their back knee, bend the front knee slightly, bend forward slightly at the waist, and swing smoothly. There is a valuable lesson in this simple stance. It contributes to balance, pivot rather than sway, smooth swing, and follow through, and, most important, it promotes consistency in technique.

I am frequently asked by people attending my shooting clinics how far forward they should lean at the waist. A good rule of thumb is to lean forward until your nose is above the toes of your front foot. Another regular inquiry is how far apart their feet should be. I would suggest that the feet be located directly under the armpits.

A common mistake among new skeet shooters is that they position their feet toward the house from which the target is thrown rather than toward where they will break the target. There are several rituals which, if performed on every shot, are conducive to shooting consistently high scores. Here they are.

Target Break Zone

As soon as you step onto the station, decide where you want to break the target and position your feet correctly to break the target in that location.

Foot Position

This can be very confusing to a new shooter. It is really rather simple. You want to have your feet positioned so that your body is able to pivot through the target break point without binding up. If you point your gun at the intended target break point and adjust your feet so that you are comfortable, you will probably be pretty close to right. Another little trick that works rather well is to have an imaginary line from you to where you want to break the target. This line should pass through the heel of your rear foot and the toes of your front foot.

3-2, 3-3, 3-4

Junior All-American Sporting Clays shooter Brian Ash demonstrates correct foot alignment with the target break point. A straight line from the heel of the rear foot and passing through the toes of the front foot should point directly toward the target break point (*3-2*). **This foot position creates a "swing window" which allows the shooter to swing both left** (*3-3*) **and right** (*3-4*) **of the target break point if necessary.** *Photo:* Gil Ash

Gun Hold Point

Once the target break zone and foot position have been established, the barrels are then pointed to the gun hold point.

The gun hold point will vary for different targets and will not be exactly the same for every shooter. Specific locations for gun hold points will be addressed in the section on how to shoot each station. Some shooters mount their guns with the barrels pointing directly at the gun hold point. Others mount their guns with the barrels pointing at the target break zone and then pivot their whole body back toward the trap house until they are pointing the barrels at the gun hold point. I prefer the latter because it seems to help me swing better if I wind my body back toward the trap house. Some experienced shooters who know their correct foot position exactly will often eliminate the step of pointing their guns at the target break point and swinging back toward the trap house. They get the correct foot position and then mount their gun directly at the gun hold point. This eliminates expending the energy it takes to swing the mounted gun back toward the house. I think it is better for new shooters to mount on the target break point and then swing back toward the trap house because it helps reinforce good form and technique.

Before swinging back to my gun hold point I make sure my stance is correct. I bend my left knee, since I am right-handed, and lock my right knee. I also check to be sure that my weight is shifted to my left leg.

Be sure your muzzles are under the target's line of flight when you are pointing at your gun hold point. As I cover each specific skeet station I will suggest a gun hold point. I will also frequently suggest that you keep your gun hold point under the target's line of flight. Frequent repetition of this suggestion is not an oversight, it is intentional. A sure way to get into trouble is to let any skeet target get lower than your muzzles.

Gun Mount

You will see a variety of gun mounts on a skeet field. Some are rather flashy, others are deliberate and may be accompanied by several precise adjustments of cheek to comb. You may even see some shooters call for targets while the gun is still dismounted and off the shoulder. The most important factor in gun mount is that it is mounted in the same place every time.

I would encourage the new shooter to learn to mount the gun by bringing the stock up to his face, rather than placing the recoil pad to his shoulder and then bringing his face down to make contact with the stock. The latter allows too many possibilities for inconsistency and poor form.

Until you are mounting the gun to the same place every time, you are in essence duplicating what a rifle shooter would be doing if he changed his rear sight on every shot. You can imagine the sorry groups that would produce!

Gale Davis is a very good skeet shooter who shoots with a dismounted gun. He is also an excellent sporting clays shooter. Years of shooting skeet with a dismounted gun may have contributed to his success in sporting clays, which require a dismounted gun when you call for a target.

Eye Focal Point

Now that the feet, body and gun are in the correct location, the eyes must be focused to see the target when it appears. Where you focus your eyes will vary for the different stations and each station will be addressed individually later. There are several general rules of thumb. It is a good idea to see the target as soon as possible. Some fields have backgrounds that make it difficult to see certain targets as they leave the target opening. In an effort to see these hard-to-see targets sooner, many inexperienced shooters look closer and closer and focus tighter and tighter on the target opening. This can make some targets even harder to see. If a target emerges with a background of vegetation or other landscape, it can be very difficult to see. These are usually low-house targets viewed from station 5 or 6. For most of us with average eyesight it is usually better to look slightly out from the target opening and have your eyes more in a wide-angle focus than in a narrow-focus, tunnel-like mode.

See the Correct Lead

Most experienced skeet shooters use the sustained-lead method on the majority of shots. Some targets are shot using the swing-through method and some require no lead at all. But sustained lead is the one used almost exclusively on low 1, low 2, high and low 3, high and low 4, high and low 5, high 6, and high 7. High 2 and low 6 are about evenly divided between those who use sustained lead and the rest of us, who must hedge our bets on these deceptive targets with the swing-through method. High and low 8 are swing-through shots. You don't have time to see these targets come out of the house, pull ahead, and see a lead before they have passed over your head and are gone. This leaves high 1, which is going directly away from you and requires no lead; just shoot at the bottom edge. Low 7 is another target that goes directly away from you and is one you can shoot directly at, unless the wind is doing weird things.

If you ask ten good skeet shooters how much lead they see using sustained lead on a specific target you will probably get several answers—and they will all be right! A person's perception of how much lead he sees when he tries to express it in feet and inches can be misleading. One guy may say he sees a two-foot lead and another will say he sees a four-foot lead and they both are seeing the same space between barrels and target. Any suggestions about how much sustained lead you should see would be approximations at best. There are no absolutes when it comes to exact gun hold points, target break points, and leads. The suggestions I make in this book are just that—suggestions.

My good friend Ed Scherer, who has two excellent videos on skeet shooting, has a neat trick for teaching people what to see on each target. He places a stack of fifteen to twenty targets at the target crossing point, then he places a stack forty inches from either side of the first stack and under the target path. Now no matter which station you are on, you can look at those targets and get an idea of approximately what the lead should look like. If you want to know what the lead is for the low house, just look at the space between the center target stack and the other stack on that side of the field.

In many cases a new shooter or one with limited experience will be seeing the correct lead, but may be doing something else that causes him to miss targets. Too many uninformed shooters think the only reason they miss is because they didn't see the right lead. Lessons from a qualified instructor are the best way to learn about all the parts that contribute to making high scores consistently.

Tip: Upper Body Integrity

Consistency is a skeet shooter's best friend. The shooter who will spend the time, money, and effort to learn the correct technique for each station and then perform that technique consistently will be a regular winner.

One of the most common technique faults is not maintaining upper body position, which requires that the head, dominant eye, stock, and barrels maintain a consistent relationship during the entire process of breaking a skeet target. This begins the very instant the target is seen until the follow through has been completed.

The easiest way to accomplish this is to transform the body from the waist up into a fixed turret, not unlike the turret on a military tank. How do you do this? By keeping your face firmly against the comb of the stock, the recoil pad positioned firmly on your shoulder, and swinging the gun by pivoting the upper body rather than just pushing or pulling the gun across in front of your stationary body.

Tracking a target with your whole upper body is conducive to keeping everything aligned, dominant eye, stock, barrels, and target.

Now you know the secrets of mastering skeet—foot position, stance, gun hold point, gun mount, eye focal point, and seeing the correct lead. There are a few other ingredients for success, such as keeping your head on the stock and developing a smooth swing and follow through.

And there are a few social rules that ought to be adhered to if you don't want to spend your whole life shooting as a one-man squad.

Avoid talking when others are shooting or preparing to shoot. Don't walk to the next station before all shooters are finished. Keep your gun open at all times unless on station and ready to shoot. Don't harvest empty hulls while you are shooting.

Tip: Windy Days

Wind can have a significant effect on any clay target. Anytime you have a strong wing blowing directly from the high house to the low house or vice versa, you can expect changes in normal target behavior. First, keep your mind right: The wind is blowing for everyone, not just you. Forget the wind, focus on the target.

If the wind is blowing from the high house toward the low house, expect the high-house targets to move a little faster and possibly be pushed down by the wind. When the wind is in this direction, you can expect the low house to rise higher and slow down faster. This type of wind usually affects low-house targets the most.

If the wind is in the opposite direction, blowing from the low house toward the high house, expect the high house to slow down and the low house to speed up and not rise as high as usual. It is easy to get in trouble by having your muzzles too high on your gun hold point when calling for low-house targets on stations 4, 5, 6, and 7. It is also easy for low-house targets to get below your barrels when shooting doubles on stations 1, 2, 3, and 4.

Schedule a few practice sessions on windy days to get some experience shooting wind-blown targets.

How To Shoot Each Station

Station 1

Since station 1 is always shot first, it is a good policy to make a final check on your safety, barrel selector, and eye and ear protection as you approach this station. I speak from experience when I say it is embarrassing and detrimental to your concentration to realize you don't have your earplugs in until after you shoot at the high-house single with your 12 gauge.

Get a good look at this target before you shoot it. If you are the first person in the squad, you have the right to view a high, a low, and a pair before you shoot. Observe closely and determine two important facts—angle and elevation. Is the target flying inside or outside the center stake? How high is it when it reaches the stake? Knowing the answers to these questions will allow you to select the correct gun hold point.

Station One—High House

Target Break Point: Break this one just before it reaches the center stake. Too much delay and deliberation will result in a much more difficult target if you shoot it too late. Wind can also make this target difficult if you let it lose too much velocity before you shoot it.

Foot Position: Mount your gun and point it about 45 degrees up over the center stake. Adjust you feet so you are comfortable. Make sure you are directly under the target opening. I have seen some people get on the extreme edges of this station for some unknown reason. Why increase the difficulty by adding another angle to the shot? Bend the front knee and distribute your weight 60/40 with 60 percent on the front foot.

Station 1—High House. Point your gun at the stake and then raise it about fifteen feet above the stake. Roll your eyes up to see the target early. Shoot it before it reaches the stake and shoot it right away.

Gun Hold Point: Mount your gun and point it directly at the center stake; now elevate it to about 15 feet over the center stake. Your gun hold point may be moved slightly right or left based on what you observed when viewing the targets. If you do your homework on this target and have a good idea where it is flying, you won't have to do much adjusting when it is in the air.

Tip: Look At High-1: Don't be lulled into a false sense of security just because you have closely observed this target. There may be a wind blowing from your left to right that blows the target to the right of the center stake, but it suddenly stops as you call for the target. Now you are expecting a target to the right of center, which you don't get. You have to focus on every target and react to what you see. This could be said for every clay target thrown.

Eye Focal Point: With your face firmly against the stock, roll your eyes upward as high as you can without discomfort. If you have a bill or brim on your hat, tip it back on your head so it won't obstruct your vision. You want to see this target as soon as possible while keeping your head firmly on the stock.

Lead: Most people let this target rest right on top of the barrels, or as some folks say, "Shoot his legs off." You will need to see just a little daylight between the target and the barrels if you shoot it late. Don't look at your gun when shooting this or any other target. If you have to shoot slightly under the target because you waited too long, focus on the target and not the barrels.

Common mistakes: Some people lift their heads in an effort to see this target early and shoot over the target. This is one shot where the head must absolutely stay down.

Station One—Low House

Station 1 low house is one of the easiest targets to break in skeet. When this one is missed it is due to mental error rather than being unable to perform the relatively easy athletic functions necessary to dust the target.

Gun Hold Point: About one-third of the way from the center stake back toward the low house. It is very easy to get your muzzles up too high on this gun hold point. Make sure you keep them below the flight of the target.

Eye Focal Point: Just to the left of the target opening.

Target Break Point: Just after it crosses the center stake, certainly no later than halfway between the center stake and the high house.

Lead: If you execute a good sustained lead and keep your barrels moving you will only need to see a six- to eight-inch lead on this target.

Common Mistakes: A gun hold point too far out from the house causes the shooter to wait too long before starting to swing,

Station 1—Low House. Gun hold point is about one third of the way from the center stake to the low house. Shoot it just after it crosses the stake for optimal pattern performance.

resulting in not enough swing, and shooting behind the target with a "dead gun."

Some shooters do just the opposite and begin swinging on the target much too early. Consequently they get way out in front as the target comes across the field and must either stop their swing or slow it drastically, resulting again in shooting behind.

Another common error is riding this target too long. It is tempting to mount your gun and ride the target all the way across the field with your swing getting slower and slower. The result is, you won't be able to resist the temptation of flicking your eyes back and forth between the target and barrels, and a miss.

Keep most of your weight over your front foot and pivot. Avoid leaning or swaying.

Station One—Doubles

There is actually no such thing as doubles in skeet. You just have two singles in the air at the same time. Shoot these targets just like the singles, with one minor adjustment. You will want to set your foot position to break the second target about halfway between the center stake and the high house. A foot position that strictly favors the high-house target may not allow enough body movement to follow through on the incoming low-house target.

Station 2—High House

While low 2 is one of the easiest shots for new shooters to master, high 2 is one of the first targets new shooters have a lot of trouble with. This target presents optical illusions and is somewhat of a trick shot. When it first comes out of the house it appears to be traveling 500 miles an hour from left to right at a 90-degree angle. By the time a shooter sees it, starts his swing, and catches it, the target is near the center stake at an angle of less than 15 degrees and requires very little, if any lead. The key

Station 2—High House. Gun hold point is parallel to the face of the target house. Cut your eyes back to the left and look just in front of the opening.

to mastering this target is gun hold point. For most people, and all new shooters, the gun hold point should never be closer to the target opening than having the barrels parallel to the side of the trap house.

Target Break Point: This target should be broken just before it reaches the center stake. Some new shooters may have to break it at the stake and then gradually work on breaking it a little quicker as they become more experienced.

Gun Hold Point: The barrels should be parallel to the side of the trap house. If a shooter is still having trouble catching and breaking this target, then the barrels can be moved slightly toward the center stake until the correct hold point is determined. If you are shooting one of the heavier-tubed over-and-unders, you will also need to move your hold point a little closer to the center stake. The muzzles should be even with the bottom of the target opening.

Eye Focal Point: Shift your eyes back toward the target opening and look just outside the opening.

Lead: I teach new shooters to shoot this with a swing-through shot without seeing any lead. Less-experienced skeet shooters have a lot of trouble keeping their barrels out in front of this target and getting a consistent sustained lead on it. With the swing-through lead, it is okay if the target jumps them and gets past the muzzles. Now all they have to do is catch it and shoot right at it. After gaining some experience and confidence on this target, you might want to learn to shoot it with a 6- to 8-inch sustained lead.

Tips: Gun Hold Point: If this target continues to give you problems, experiment with moving your gun hold point slightly toward the center stake. Avoid holding your gun too high when calling for this target. If you get it above the bottom of the target opening you are too high.

Tip: Lead: There is a tendency for shooters to lead this target too much. Even when shooters shoot behind the target it is because they were fooled by the illusion of the target going faster than it really was. They get way out in front of it, stop the gun, and shoot behind. To make matters worse, when their buddy tells them they are behind, they get farther in front, stop the gun again, and the cycle is repeated. Remember—very little or no lead and keep swinging.

Station 2—Low House

This is the very first station I choose to begin teaching a brand new, right-handed shooter. It requires all the principal ingredients of all skeet shots: head down, swing through, and see a sustained lead. These basics are easier to learn and execute on this target. Since it is an easy shot to master, it quickly builds confidence. I begin new, left-handed shooters on high 6.

Station 2—Low House. Gun hold point is one third of the way back from the center stake toward the low house and slightly under the target flight path.

Target Break Point: Just after it crosses the center stake to get optimum pattern performance. If you shoot this target here it will not have slowed down enough to be affected much by wind or gravity. Some people like to ride this target and really smokeball it just before it goes past the high house. The black puffs of smoke are unbelievable—so are the occasional misses. When you ride any skeet target, you increase the chances of error.

Gun Hold Point: One-third of the way from the crossing stake back toward the low house and slightly under the target's line of flight.

Eye Focal Point: Look just to the left of the target opening.

Sustained Lead: You should only have to see a very slight lead of about six inches on this target if you shoot it where I suggest.

Bend your front knee and keep most of your weight on the front foot. It is very easy to shift your weight to your back foot and begin to sway on this target. Keep weight forward and pivot, don't sway. This target appears to be extremely slow after shooting high 2. Don't allow yourself to be lulled into complacency, follow through.

Tip: No Easy Shots: Low 1, low 2, high 6, and high 7 are targets that are often missed because they are too easy. All four of these targets are incomers that give you lots of time and require very little lead. Don't go to sleep. Avoid the temptation to ride this shot. When the lead is right, break the target and swing through. The only easy ones are the ones you break!

Station 2—Doubles

The high house is shot exactly as the single. The only exception would be to move your foot position back toward the high house slightly to give yourself enough swing for the second target coming out of the low house. This adjustment in foot position is slight, as too much shifting toward the high house could cause you to bind up on the outgoing first target.

For some shooters, the second target in doubles on stations 2 through 6 is shot with a come-from-behind, swing-through lead. The swing-through lead on the second target will be slightly less than what you see when you shoot it as a single. Keep your head on the comb and keep swinging the gun.

Station 3—High House

This target can get the jump on you if you are not alert when you call for it. You can also get in trouble if you anticipate it and start your swing before you see it come out of the target opening. Be ready, but see it before you start your swing.

As soon as you see this target emerge, begin your swing and pivot with a smooth start. Don't panic and get too far in front of it with a frantic first move. Like its cousin, high 2, it can be deceptive and appear to be moving faster than it really is because of your proximity to the house and the hard angle.

Station 3—High House. Gun hold point is two thirds of the way back from the center stake toward the high house.

Target Break Point: This one should be broken right over or just before the center stake. It is easy to ride this target too long and shoot behind it. The key to making a sustained lead work is to keep the gun moving at the same speed as the target.

Gun Hold Point: About two-thirds of the way from the center stake back toward the high house. Keep the barrels below the target opening and the target line of flight.

Eye Focal Point: Look to the left of your barrels and just outside of the target opening.

Sustained Lead: About eighteen inches.

Tip: Jumping the Target: You will miss some of these because the target jumped you and you were late starting your swing. You will also probably miss some because you anticipated the target and jumped too far out in front of it. It is important to see the target before you swing. It is equally important to begin your swing smoothly and pivot the instant you see the target. If you work on this aspect of shooting high 3, your scores here will improve dramatically.

Station 3—Low House

This target, along with high 5, shares the distinction of requiring the longest sustained lead of all skeet targets. Many casual skeet shooters think station 4 requires the longest leads but that is not true. When low 3 and high 5 are passing through the target break zone over the center stake they are traveling at 90-degree angles to your station, which requires the greatest forward allowance.

Target Break Point: Directly over the center stake or slightly past.

Gun Hold Point: About halfway between the center stake and the low house. Keep the muzzles just below the target flight path.

Eye Focal Point: Just outside the target opening.

Station 3—Low House. This target, along with high 5, requires the longest sustained lead on the skeet field. Gun hold point is about two thirds of the way from the center stake to the low house. Avoid the temptation to ride this target.

Sustained Lead: Three to 3½ feet. Start a smooth swing and pivot as soon as you see the target.

Tip: Shoot Near the Center Stake

Because this target requires so much sustained lead, many shooters try to be too careful and begin to check and measure their lead. This leads to disaster. The lead for this target can change drastically if you ride it very far past the center stake.

All low-house targets are climbing. Consequently, because they are fighting gravity all the way across the field, they begin to slow dramatically when they get about halfway between the center stake and the high house. To prove this, stand on station 1 and have someone throw several low-house targets for you and observe the decrease in trajectory. Keep your head down and follow through.

Station 4

As I mentioned in the section on station 3, many shooters erroneously believe the two targets on station 4 require the longest leads of all targets. If you work on your gun hold points and learn to break them over or just before the center stake, you will only need to see a sustained lead of one-and-one-half to two feet. As with most of the other targets in this game, you need to keep that swing moving and follow through.

Station 4—High House

Target Break Point: Over or near the center stake. The lead for both of these targets is the same if you break them in the middle of the field or just before the center stake. If you follow the low house much past the center stake it will begin to slow just enough to make you miss.

Station 4—High House. Gun hold point is about halfway between the center stake and the high house.

Gun Hold Point: About halfway between the high house and the center stake with the muzzles just below the target flight path.

Eye Focal Point: Just outside the target opening.

Sustained Lead: One-and-one-half to two feet is about right for this target. Start your swing as soon as the target emerges.

Tip: Focus On Target

As is the case with most clay targets that are relatively far away from the shooter, there is a tendency on station 4 to want to make sure of your lead and flick your eyes back to your gun. Time after time I have had students stop or drastically slow a beautiful swing and perfect lead to check and measure where their gun barrels were. The outcome is always the same—they miss. How many times have you had someone behind you say, "You stopped your gun." You are usually surprised by this statement since you had no conscious intention of stopping your swing. In all likelihood, you didn't intentionally stop your swing—you looked at your barrels. The slowing and stopping of your swing was a byproduct of looking at your gun. The target is always in sharp focus. Forward allowance when using sustained lead is determined by focusing on the target and only seeing the gun barrels out of focus in your peripheral vision.

Tip: Wood On Wood

It is very easy for left-handers to lift their heads on this target, especially if they have the muzzles too high at the gun hold point. Right-handers have the same problem on low 4.

Station 4—Low House

Just about everything said for high 4 applies to low 4 as well. When you have difficulty with one of these targets it is usually because of whether, you shoot left-handed or right-handed, or you don't get your muzzles below the target flight path when pointing to your gun hold point. Right-handers swing more easily and smoothly to their left. When righties swing toward the left, this causes the stock to move toward the face, which contributes to keeping "wood on wood."

Target Break Point: Over the center stake.

Gun Hold Point: About halfway between the center stake and the low house. Don't get your barrels too high; keep them just under the target flight path.

Eye Focal Point: Just outside the target opening.

Sustained Lead: One-and-one-half to two feet. Begin your swing as soon as you see the target come out of the house.

Station 4—Low House. Gun hold point is about halfway between the low house and the center stake. Be careful not to get your gun hold point too high on low 4.

Station 5—Low House. Gun hold point is about two thirds of the way from the center stake toward the low house.

Tip: Don't Peep: It is very tempting for right-handers to lift their heads off the stock on this target, especially if your barrels are below the target flight path when you call for the target. This is not a contradiction to the previous statement about right-handers swinging more easily to the left and being able to keep their heads down, because the stock is being moved toward the face. The head lifting on low-house targets is due to the barrels being too high and having targets dip under them. If the high house were on the right side of the field, I doubt right-handers would ever take their heads off their stocks.

Station 5

Like its little brother, low 3, high 5 requires the longest lead on the field. Right-handers must keep firm contact with face against stock, since the gun is swinging away from the face on this target.

Station 5—High House

Target Break Point: Shoot this one right over the crossing point or slightly after.

Gun Hold Point: About two-thirds of the way from the center stake to the high house. Barrels should be no higher than the bottom of the target opening.

Eye Focal Point: Look right at the target opening.

Sustained Lead: High 5 along with low 3 require the longest leads in skeet. See three to three-and-one-half feet on this target. Start a smooth swing as soon as you see the target.

Tip: Avoiding Swaying On High 5

It is tempting to sway and lean on high 5, especially when the shooter is right-handed. Most high 5 targets are missed because the shooter either swayed rather than pivoted or swung the gun with just the arms. Make sure your feet are positioned correctly so your body doesn't bind up and slow your swing.

Another factor that can contribute to swaying on this shot is having your feet too far apart—shoulder width is about right for most shooters. A good way to insure a good pivot is to begin to pivot as soon as you see the target emerge from the trap house opening.

Station 5—Low House

One of the more common mistakes I see on low 5 is a gun hold point that is too high. If the barrels are pointed too high you will either swing through the target at an oblique angle, rather than swinging through on the target's line of flight, or, worse still, it will pass under your barrels. It is important to have the barrels just under the target's line of flight when calling for the target on all stations, but it is most important on low 5 and low 6.

Station 5—High House. Gun hold point is about two thirds of the way from the center stake toward the high house.

This can be a difficult target to see if there is a bad background. If it frequently gets the jump on you, move both your visual focal point and gun hold point out slightly away from the low house.

Target Break Point: Just before or right over the center stake.

Gun Hold Point: About two-thirds of the way from the center stake to the low house. Keep the muzzles under the target flight line.

Eye Focal Point: Look right in the target opening.

Sustained Lead: Two to two-and-one-half feet. Since this target follows high 5, which requires the longest sustained lead in skeet, it is easy to overlead this target or get too far in front and get caught with a dead gun.

Station 6

Station 6 mirrors station 2, with only a few differences. It is important to know what they are. The outgoing low house is often launched against a cluttered background, making it difficult to see. If a bad background makes the low-house target hard to see, you may want to bring your eye focal point out, away from the target opening slightly. Don't get lazy on high 6. Keep your gun swinging and pivot—don't sway.

Station 6—High House

Target Break Point: One-third of the way from the center stake back toward the low house.

Gun Hold Point: One-third of the way from the center stake back toward the high house.

Eye Focal Point: Look right at the target opening.

3-K

Station 6—High House. Gun hold point is one third of the way from the center stake back toward the high house.

Sustained Lead: Only about six inches.

Station 6—Low House

You must start swinging as soon as you see this target emerge. Work on breaking this target with a short, sustained lead of three to six inches. This will look like about one-half of a target. It would also be wise to learn to shoot this target with a swing-through lead. I have run hot and cold on this target and high 2, which is basically the same shot, so often that I shoot it almost all the time as a swing-through target and shoot right at it over the center stake.

Target Break Point: Break this target slightly before or right at the stake.

Gun Hold Point: Parallel to the side of the low house or just a few degrees to the left of parallel.

Eye Focal Point: Look to the right of your gun barrels about halfway back to the target opening.

Station 6—Low House. Gun hold point is parallel with the face of the trap house. Be careful not to hold your barrels too high when calling for this target.

Sustained Lead: See about three to six inches with a sustained lead. You won't have a lot of time to admire this lead or ride the target to check or measure.

Swing-Through Lead: If this target jumps you and you have to resort to a swing-through lead, it will already have passed your muzzles, so swing through it and shoot right at it. Your muzzle speed will be great enough to provide what little forward allowance you need on this shot.

Tip: Horizontal Muzzles

To avoid getting a gun hold point that is too high, try calling for a few targets while holding your gun perfectly horizontal. Don't swing at the target, just watch the elevation of the target as it passes by your muzzles. I think you will see that this is about the right muzzle elevation for most shooters to stay just under the target's line of flight.

Station 6—Doubles

Don't rush the low-house target. Shoot it just like a single and see it break before shifting your eyes to the high house. Remember, there are no doubles in skeet, just two singles flying at the same time. You can only break one target at a time so concentrate on one at a time. It isn't rare for a shooter to miss both targets because he hurried the low house, missed it, and then missed the high house because he was thinking about having just missed the low house. You can't worry about the next target, or the last one, or anything else that might be going on: You have to focus on breaking the target that is in the air.

You may want to favor the second target's break point by adjusting your foot position slightly to the right. Don't shift so much that you retard your swing on the outgoing low-house target. This is a matter of inches and a hard thing to specify. After a little experimentation you will be able to determine what is best for your timing and swing.

Station 7

"There are no easy targets!" It is easy to relax and not focus on every target after leaving station 6. When you leave station 6, you have put most of those targets behind you that cost people 100 straight or 25 straight. Many a championship has been lost because a shooter stepped onto station 7 thinking his work was done. Station 7 can be very hard, simply because it is so easy.

Station 7—High House

Target Break Point: Take this one just after it passes over the center stake about one-third of the way to the low house.

Gun Hold Point: About one-third of the way back from the center stake toward the high house.

Station 7—High House. Gun hold point is about one third of the way from the center stake back toward the high house.

Station 7—Low House. Point the barrels right at the crossing stake and then raise the barrels up about twelve feet. Your barrels will be slightly above horizontal. You can determine how high to hold for both low 7 and high 1 by having someone hold the hoop which is used for checking correct target heights at the crossing stake. Now you can see how high you should hold on these two outgoing targets.

The mark of a good skeet shooter: the shot has been fired, the gun has recoiled, the autoloader has ejected the empty, and Gale Davis still has his face firmly against the stock.

Eye Focal Point: See the target come out of the opening.

Sustained Lead: About three to six inches. Keep your swing going and follow through.

Station 7—Low House

Target Break Point: Slightly before or right over the center stake.

Gun Hold Point: Point right at the stake and then raise your barrels up to about twelve feet. If targets are being blown to left or right of the center stake, you may want to favor that side of the stake slightly with your gun hold point.

Eye Focal Point: Look slightly to the right of your barrels.

Tips: Wood On Wood: Keep your face firmly into the stock. It is tempting to lift your head as this target is going away from you and rising. Don't shoot this one too quickly. Concentrate on the target and break it just before it reaches the center stake. A new shooter may have to wait until it gets over the center stake, but as you gain more experience you should work on breaking it a little sooner.

Station 7—Doubles

Both of these targets can be shot exactly as they were as singles. Don't rush the first shot. See the low-house target turn to smoke and then cut your eyes toward the incomer. Don't go to sleep on this second target. Keep your barrels moving.

Station 8

Everything I said about relaxing at station 7 also applies here at 8. It is easy to assume your work is over and your 100 straight is in the score book. I have also seen 100 straights lost on station 8 because the shooter choked. Either extreme in mental focus can be disastrous. The solution to this dilemma is to shoot this station just like all the others—one target at a time. Don't think about your score or anything else but breaking the target that is in the air. You can practice developing this mindset as part of your training regimen. Just imagine you are at the World Shoot, three targets away from tying Mayes and Bender and going to the shoot-offs. The more you do this the more realistic it will become.

In spite of the speed required to break these station 8 targets, they are fairly easy to master as far the athletic part goes. It is the mental portion of this target that can make it tough. You can't hesitate or start too soon. Learn to let your mind go blank and react to the target when it comes out of the house and you will do well on station 8.

Tip: Learning To Break Station 8: If you have trouble with either target on station 8, back up about ten yards behind the station and learn to break the target. Then move about half the distance toward the station and shoot it some more. Your next move is

Station 8—High House. Gun hold point is one yard right of bottom right hand corner of the target opening.

onto the station, where you will be breaking them with the same regularity as you did ten yards behind the station

Station 8—High House

Target Break Point: Two-thirds of the way from high house to center stake.

Gun Hold Point: I will give you two options here. I have had students do well with both. One option is one yard to the right of the bottom right-hand corner of the trap opening (this one works best for me). The other is Ed Scherer's method of one foot over and one foot up from the upper right-hand corner of the target opening.

Eye Focal Point: There are no options here; look into the opening and see the target come out of the house.

Swing Through Lead: There are some who profess to see and hold a sustained lead on station 8, and they may be telling the

Station 8—Low House. Gun hold point is about one yard left of the top left-hand corner of the target opening. I hope you always shoot two on low 8.

truth. It is all I can do to see the target and catch it, much less see and maintain a lead. As soon as you see the target emerge, start swinging, and as soon as you cover it up, pull the trigger. Some shooters insist they shoot the front edge of these targets.

Station 8—Low House

Target Break Point: One-half to two-thirds of the way from the low house to the center stake.

Gun Hold Point: Top left-hand corner of target opening and out about a yard.

Eye Focal Point: Look to the right and over your barrels.

Swing Through Lead: Start your swing as soon as you see the target emerge. Swing through it and pull the trigger as you cover it up.

Tip: Where To Stand

To set yourself up properly to break this target, get as far back in the pad as possible, move to the far inside of the pad (away from the center stake), position your feet so you can mount your gun, and point it fifteen feet over the center stake. Now, with your gun mounted, wind yourself back toward your hold point. By swinging in reverse, you set yourself up to make a good move on the target. I see more shooters set up incorrectly for station 8 targets than all the other stations combined.

I hope you always shoot two on the station 8 low house!

Doubles At Stations 3, 4, and 5

If you shoot tournaments long enough, sooner or later you will end up paired with someone else or a with a whole bunch of folks, to determine a winner in a doubles shoot-off at stations 3, 4, and 5. This tie-breaker was devised to shorten the extensive shoot-offs that occurred when champion skeet shooters broke ties by shooting the standard round of skeet. Shoot-offs at the World Championships literally lasted for days.

A good way to practice doubles at 3, 4, and 5 is to shoot a few regular rounds of skeet, or a practice session, and then break for awhile. After taking a break, come back to the field and practice shooting doubles at 3, 4, and 5 as in a shoot-off. You will learn first-hand what it is like to shoot several rounds, get cold, and then have to come back to shoot in a miss-and-out environment.

Station 3—Doubles

Shoot the high house like you did as a single, and see it break. Don't rush the first shot. If you don't break the first one, you can't break a pair. The second shot will probably be a swing-through, requiring you to see somewhat less of a lead than you see when shooting the single with a sustained lead. Surprisingly, many shooters miss the second target in doubles by shooting in front of it. If you are consistently missing the low house off this station, shorten your lead a little. You will be surprised.

Station 4—Doubles

High House First

When advancing around the field from station 3 toward 5, you shoot the high house first on station 4. When you are coming back the other way, you shoot the low house first.

If you shoot the high house slightly before the center stake or right over it, your barrels will be in good position to swing through the low-house target and break it. If you rush the high-house target (or any first target in doubles) you will be way out in front of the second target with a dead gun and no room to execute a decent swing. When you get caught way out in front of your second target like this, your only option is the snap shot, which does not yield much target dust.

Station 4—Low House First

Again, shoot the first target just like the single. See it break and then cut your eyes to the high house and swing through it. Be careful to get your muzzles below the low-house target line of flight in your gun hold position.

Station 5—Doubles

Shoot the low-house target just like the single, and see it break, then cut your eyes to the incoming high-house target. Keep your face firmly against the stock. The lead will be slightly less on the high house than when you shot it as a single.

It is a good idea to work on making your second doubles shot as fast as your improving skill level allows. If you attend a major skeet tournament, you will see that the best doubles shooters break the targets in almost the same spot. They didn't start off breaking them that fast, but they worked hard to develop this ability.

Tips:

Make sure your gun hold point is below the flight path of the first target coming out of the low house. Having your gun hold point too high could cause you to attempt the target too late or lift your head in an effort to see it. Either error could be responsible for losing one or both of the pair.

Remember that old skeet shooting admonition, "There is no such thing as doubles—just two singles in the air at the same time." You must break them one at the time. You must focus visually and mentally on each target if you are to have any success at doubles.

Focus on the first target visually and mentally. Shoot at the first target, then focus on the second target. It is quite common for a shooter to miss his first bird of a pair and then miss the second because he is mentally focused on the unpleasant fact that he missed the first one.

Don't rush the first shot. Rushing the first shot often results in both targets being missed. Rushing a shot at any target will often cause you to miss it. If that target is the first of a pair, it could also cause you to have a "dead gun" and miss the second. The dead gun in this case is created when you attempt the first target too early, resulting in your muzzles being pointed too near the low house to allow for any appreciable swing on the high-house target that will be crossing left to right.

Common Mistakes:

Avoid the tendency to roll your shoulders on the second target as it comes across the field. The longer you ride this target to be absolutely sure the lead is correct, the more apt you are to roll your shoulders and shoot under the target.

It is very tempting to lift your head in an effort to see the second target. Resist the temptation to "peep."

Many shooters shoot over the second bird on doubles because it has started to fall by the time they shoot. Take it earlier or shoot their legs off. In other words, float the target slightly by having the muzzles a little more below the target than when you shoot them at the crossing stake.

Tip: Sustained vs. Swing-Through On the Second Target: Some very good shooters use both methods. In teaching I have found that shooters will swing through the second target with a positive move, whereas when they try to see a sustained lead and maintain it, the target gets away from them.

Sporting Clays

This game originated in the 1920s in Great Britain for the purpose of teaching wingshooting skills to wealthy sportsmen. In the last seventy years, it has expanded worldwide and become recognized as not only a system for teaching wingshooting skills, but also as a tournament sport and one of the major recreational clay target shooting sports.

The growth in the number of sporting clays courses understandably has paralleled the sport's unbelievable growth in popularity among shotgunners. We have seen courses built from scratch, and farmers install sporting clays machines on unused acres or just set up a few machines on the weekends. Many hunting preserves have added sporting clays facilities for teaching wingshooting, additional cash flow during hunting season, and as a major activity when hunting season is closed. Many resorts have added sporting clays as an additional activity. I am also told of another indicator of the increased favor of sporting clays in America: Several clubs where I teach clinics have told me that business travelers from out of town are bringing their shotguns along and shooting with clients rather than playing golf. And I have companies booking one-day shooting clinics for their clients rather than going to a golf course.

The growing interest in sporting clays has spawned some very interesting events including the Holland Sporting Clays week in Vail, Colorado. This week-long event features top shooting instructors from both England and the United States. Eight of the shooters in this photo attended the year before and had so much fun that they came back again.

Statistics indicate that the large majority of sporting clays shooters are recreational shooters who shoot once or twice a month and hunters who enjoy sporting clays during the off season to sharpen wingshooting skills prior to the season opening. And there are several thousand serious competitive shooters who participate in registered tournaments. The charity tournaments sponsored by conservation organizations such as Ducks Unlimited and Quail Unlimited draw large numbers of shooters across the country.

The Sporting Clays Course

Unlike other clay shooting games that are built to rigid dimensions and specifications, sporting clays courses are designed to

It is fairly common knowledge that serious competitors take lessons
and practice with a shooting coach. This pair of mother and son
sporting clays All Americans are a good example. More and more
clubs throughout the country are offering clinics for shooters at all
levels. A list of instructors is located in the appendix of this book.
Add an extra dimension to your club and contact one of these
instructors to give a few clinics and some private lessons.

blend in with the environment. This is not only aesthetically
pleasing to the shooter, it also keeps cost down. I know of some
great courses that were built with nothing but a chain saw and a
few Lincoln trap machines. If you are planing a course and expect
to spend some significant dollars, I suggest you obtain the ser-
vices of a course designer. There are several who place ads in the
sporting clays magazines. Before you come to an agreement, ask
them for a list of their clients and make a few phone calls.

A sporting clays course is divided into several fields that
usually duplicate the flight characteristics of a specific game bird.
Several traps positioned around a lake, with a shooting station
located in a duck blind, would feature the kinds of shots encoun-
tered when shooting waterfowl over decoys, with targets either
passing low overhead or curling and settling out over your decoys. Another field might feature doves, with targets launched off

a tower. The grouse and woodcock fields are usually situated in locations that feature woods, and targets angle away or cross in front. I once saw a great pheasant field built in a stand of corn that had been planted to simulate the pheasant's natural habitat. The field offered realistic shooting, with the trap machines set to throw steep, going-away shots. There wasn't a pheasant within 2,000 miles of that field, but shooters experienced what it is really like to shoot pheasants.

I have seen pit blinds that duplicated the red grouse blinds of Scotland, with incoming targets to simulate driven birds. Shooters on this field had an international shooting experience without even driving to the airport and could have bought a car with the money they saved foregoing a trip to Scotland.

Each field will contain one or more shooting stations or stands to provide a variety of shots from a minimum number of machines. A single trap machine mounted on a tower can provide just about any conceivable angle of target presentation when there are four or five shooting stations strategically placed around it.

Modern choke technology and recent improvements in shot-shell design has given the sporting clays shooter tremendous flexibility in optimal shotgun performance.

Guns

If you are shooting just for fun, any shotgun you enjoy shooting can be used. I have seen just about every gun imaginable used in this sport. If you shoot sporting clays to hone wingshooting skills for hunting season, then obviously your field gun is the right choice.

More serious participants and tournament shooters usually favor the over-and-under with interchangeable screw-in chokes. The second most popular gun among serious devotees of the sport is the autoloader. These guns usually have 28- or 30-inch barrels and are often ported.

Sporting clays guns usually have stocks approximating the dimensions used by skeet shooters. It is advisable to have a gun that shoots slightly high so that you can "float" a little bit over the barrels with a slight bit of daylight between the target and the barrels. This allows you to always see the target just above the barrels and not have to cover it up.

Chokes and Loads

If I had to select one choke-and-load combination for all sporting clays shooting, it would be improved cylinder (.010 constrictions) and a factory trap load with 1⅛ ounces of number 8s. Fortunately this is not necessary unless the shooter has a gun with fixed chokes and only enough cash for one box of shells. I have noticed with sporting clays shooters that as the degree of experience and knowledge increases so does the variety of chokes and loads.

One hallmark of a good sporting clays course is the variety of target presentation. Target presentation on a well-designed course will offer all the "specialty targets," such as battues, minis (60 mm), middies (90 mm), standards (110 mm), and rabbits. On a well-designed course, targets will be presented as singles, following pairs, report pairs, true pairs, incomers, outgoers, crossing shots from both left and right, and targets off towers. No one choke-and-load combination is ideal for all possibilities. A single choke and load is at best a compromise that will perform adequately on most targets.

I am continuously amazed at shooters who spend all sorts of money shooting sporting clays and never taking the time to pattern their guns to find out how various chokes and loads perform in their specific shotgun. I have seen shooters spend megabucks on fancy shotguns inlaid with gold peacocks, shoot thousands of practice rounds, take lessons from the best shooting instructors, pay travel and entry fees in major tournaments, and then don't have a clue as to the differences in choke and load performance in their guns at 15 or 45 yards.

Some shooters argue that they are confused by all the technical talk about constrictions, forcing cones, bore diameters, and the difference between improved cylinder and skeet chokes. All this information is fascinating to most serious shooters. But you don't need to know all the technical terms and general witchcraft practiced by the custom-barrel gurus. Neither can you completely trust the information stamped on your barrel by the factory, which denotes the choke for that barrel.

The only way you will ever know for sure which load is best at the various sporting clays distances is to pattern your gun. If you go about the process objectively, the knowledge you gain about your shotgun and how it performs will be sufficient reward for your time and effort.

Selecting Chokes and Loads: A Short Course

For those of you who just want basic information on chokes and loads I offer the following.

Shot: The majority of all clay targets will be broken with shot sizes 9, 8, and 7½. Out to 25 yards, a skeet load with a dose of number 9s will break targets. American and International skeet are games in which targets are rarely taken beyond 25 yards, and number 9 shot is the overwhelming choice of shooters who excel at this game. I never saw anyone shoot skeet with 7½ shot.

The are several different games in American trap, including 16-yard singles, handicap, and doubles. In singles, the targets are usually hit 30–35 yards from the shooter. In handicaps, depending upon the shooter's yardage handicap, targets may be taken anywhere from 35 yards to about 45 yards. Some shooters use 8s for handicaps, some use 7½s. I don't think I have ever seen anyone who had an IQ bigger than his hat size use 9s for handicap trap. As shooters get nearer and nearer the prestigious 27-yard line, 7½s are more prevalent, with 8s slightly more common at the shorter yardages.

In summary, I suggest you take a lesson from trap and skeet shooters when choosing shot size. Go with the skeet shooters when shooting targets at skeet distances, under 25 yards. For targets out to 40 yards or so, 8s will do the job as long as your chokes are tight enough to keep them flying close together. Somewhere in the neighborhood of 40 yards or so you need to begin considering the use of 7½s.

All the above statements concerning shot size are a general guide and the suggestions are based upon the assumption that your gun is properly choked to shoot targets at the distances mentioned.

Chokes: A Short Course

The same general suggestions for shot sizes are applicable for chokes used by skeet and trap shooters. Skeet shooters use several chokes, all designed to open patterns quickly for optimum dispersal at the closer ranges at which skeet targets are broken. The three most common chokes are cylinder (.000 constrictions), skeet (.005), and jug or tula chokes. A choke with about .005 constriction is probably the most commonly used on skeet fields in this country.

Since trap shooters take their targets a little farther out, chokes tend to be tighter (more constriction) than skeet chokes.

It would not be unusual to see modified, improved-modified, light-full, full, and extra-full chokes used in the singles, handicap, and doubles events at a trap shoot. Those trap shooters using the more open chokes, such as modified, are of the opinion that the somewhat larger patterns allow them to break targets they may have missed with the tighter full chokes, due to a slight pointing error. Those who advocate the tighter chokes worry about targets missed due to the thinner patterns thrown by the more open modified chokes. They are both correct. There are too many variables to establish one single choke as the best for all shooters. I repeat—this is a quick course in choke selection and therefore suggestions must be general. At trap ranges shoot the chokes trap shooters use, which would primarily be modified (.020 constriction), improved modified (.030 constriction), and full (.040).

If you do not plan to pattern your gun or don't have time before your next trip to your favorite sporting clays course, here are some very general suggestions for chokes and loads.

For targets out to 25 yards, use an open choke such as cylinder or skeet and number 9 shot. For 25 to 35 yards use improved cylinder and number 8 shot. For 35 to 45 yards, I suggest either modified or improved-modified chokes and number 8s or 7½s. For shots longer than 45 yards (there are a few around) I recommend full chokes and number 7½s trap loads. Due to variations in manufacturer's choke and barrel dimensions and your gun's individual patterning characteristics with different sized shot, these suggestions are at best approximations. You won't know for sure until you test chokes and loads at 10-yard increments.

Just a few years ago only the top competitors changed chokes during sporting clays tournaments. Now a lot of competitors have wised up, like these three, and select the correct choke for each station.

How To Shoot Sporting Clays

There are several critical skills that must be mastered if you are to achieve any significant degree of success in shooting sporting clays. You must learn to not just look at a target, but really see it and read it. You must learn the basics of gun mounting and be able to perform them consistently. You must learn to swing your shotgun through the target. If you master these skills, then everything else will fall into place. It is just that simple, but it's not easy.

A shotgun is not aimed at moving targets. It is pointed. You do not look at the bead, the rib or the barrels. You look at the *target* with maximum intensity. You are aware of the barrels only to the degree that you are aware of the front end of your car when you drive.

Did you ever hear a baseball coach tell a batter to keep his eye on the bat? Does a tennis player look at the racket when he serves? Does a carpenter look at the hammer or the nail? Now do you understand why you can't look at the gun?

If we allow our subconscious minds to function, then even the most average shooters are capable of extraordinary eye-hand coordination. If you complicate things by letting your brain attempt calculations and deliberations, then your subconscious cannot do its job.

The subconscious can be programmed to break targets in two ways and any training or learning process should include both. Your subconscious can be programmed with actual practice and also by using visualization skills. The mind is like a computer; what you put in is what you get out. Practice must be perfect. Visualization exercises must reinforce positive experiences and correct technique.

Holding the Gun

The amount of success achieved with a shotgun can be impacted by how you hold the gun. I suggest you keep your *unloaded* shotgun where it is easily accessible and pick it up several times a day and just hold it, carry it around, and mount it. It should feel like part of your body. Since you will be shooting targets by pointing it instinctively, then in reality it *is* a part of your body when you are shooting it.

The hand which holds the fore-end should have the first finger extended as illustrated in this photo. This allows you to utilize your natural pointing ability.

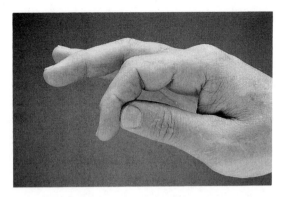

To find the sweet spot on your trigger finger, locate the portion of your forefinger which has the least amount of fleshy padding—usually just in front of the last joint. *Photo:* Gil Ash

The most important job of holding and pointing a shotgun is done with the hand that holds the fore-end. This is the hand that guides the gun and points it at the target. I suggest you extend your forefinger along the fore-end, parallel to the barrels when holding your shotgun. This hand position reinforces your ability to use your natural pointing skills.

The hand that holds the grip is also important and must be placed in the correct position. The length of your fingers and the width of your palm determine where the grip hand should be placed. First we need to establish where your trigger finger should contact the trigger.

If you apply pressure to your trigger finger just past the last joint, you will discover an area there that has very little padding or flesh. That is the surface of your finger that should touch the trigger. If you use the fleshy part of your fingertip you lose precise control of the trigger, resulting in premature or delayed trigger control.

Once this sweet spot is located on the finger, place that spot on the trigger of an empty gun and bring your hand as far back on the grip as you can while maintaining the correct finger/ trigger relationship. This is where you should put the hand that holds the grip for optimum trigger control as well as control of the stock during the gun mount and swing.

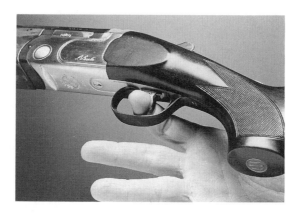

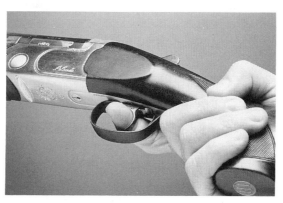

Once the sweet spot has been located, place it directly on the trigger and bring your hand as far down the grip as possible while keeping the sweet spot on the trigger. Your thumb and index finger should touch if your hand is correctly placed upon the grip. *Photo:* Gil Ash

Gun Mount

Unlike skeet and trap, when shooting sporting clays the gun is not mounted prior to calling for the target. The gun is not even mounted before you begin swinging after a target. The gun is

The gun mount should begin from the same ready position for each shot. If you tuck just one half inch of the comb under your arm, it will force you to extend the hand on the fore-end and the stock will come up to touch the face. Mounting the gun with too much force with the hand on the grip will result in a "see-saw" movement of the barrels and missed shots.

mounted during the swing. The swing and mount are performed in unison. The first move on every shot is the barrels accelerating along the path of the target. The gun is only mounted as the barrels approach the target and are about to overtake it. Only then is the comb of the stock brought up to the face and the gun fired.

The gun mount begins with using the same ready position each time, every time. Eliminating the variables in gun handling is one of the key factors in being an outstanding sporting clays shot. How can you mount consistently if you start each mount with a different ready position?

The ready position includes how you hold the gun and where the gun is placed in relation to your body. I suggest you insert about half an inch of the stock under your armpit. This will insure that the gun is in the same place before every mount. This position will also keep you "legal" in tournaments where the gun is required to be below the armpit. The arm should not clamp onto the stock, but should be slightly raised at the elbow to ensure a smooth exit.

The gun is mounted by extending the hand holding the fore-end. As the forend is extended, a gentle upward pressure lifts the comb to the face. This is important: the stock comes to the face, the face doesn't go down to the stock. The stock is not brought to the shoulder, the stock is lifted to the face. Your head should not move downward toward the stock when you mount the gun.

In addition to extending the gun so it will come out from the armpit and rise to touch the face, the fore-end hand also points the gun at the target. This is the first function of mounting the gun: The fore-end hand swings the barrels along the target line and begins to track the target. The gun is not actually mounted until the barrels begin to overtake the target and are about to pass it.

The swing is executed with the entire body, not just the arms. The upper body must maintain what is called "upper body integrity." It must pivot like the turret on a tank, maintaining the same alignment of upper body, shoulders, head, and gun barrels. All this "stuff" swings together as a single unit.

Lead

Many shotgunners experience poor results because they focus too much on seeing a specific lead. In skeet this is a practical and accepted method because you can memorize the specific sustained leads. I teach sustained leads in skeet shooting clinics. But in my sporting clays and wingshooting clinics, I don't even mention seeing a specific lead.

I encourage participants in my sporting clays clinics to shoot right at the target. When I tell students I am going to teach them to shoot moving targets without seeing a lead, they all think they have just given their money to a crazy man. I enjoy seeing the disbelief on their faces when I tell them this. And I immensely enjoy the look of disbelief when they first begin to break targets with this system.

What I am actually teaching them is a modified Churchill/ instinctive method of swing-through lead, like that taught by the Holland & Holland Shooting School in London. I have had the opportunity to teach this method not only in my clinics but also in several week-long Holland & Holland shooting clinics in Vail, Colorado.

The method is quite simple. You come from behind the target with a dismounted gun; as you overtake the target you mount the gun, shoot at the target, and follow through. The method is simple, but it takes some work to master it.

This system is broken down into several parts: target break point, gun hold point, and eye focal point. Let's take them one at a time.

Target Break Point

After viewing the target, several factors must be considered to determine the best place to break the target: distance, angle, trajectory, natural obstacles, effect of the wind, and others. Selecting the best place to break a target is a tactical decision. After selecting the break point, it is used as a basis to determine foot position, gun hold point, and eye focal point.

Once the target break point is determined, position your feet to break the target in that location. One method of aligning your feet is to project an imaginary line that passes from the heel of your rear foot to the toe of your front foot to the target break point. This foot position works for both left- and right-handers and allows some leeway if you have to take the target a little early or late. *See photo on page 56.*

Gun Hold Point

After the target break point is located and the correct foot position established, the body is wound like a spring back toward the trap machine to the gun hold point. On a 90-degree angle crossing shot the gun hold point will need to be closer to the machine than on a shot quartering away at a slight angle. Determining how close you hold back toward the machine depends on several factors including speed of the target, your visual skills, and hand speed. No two people see targets exactly the same or swing the gun at the same speed.

The gun hold point should always be just below the flight path of the target. When the gun hold point is in this position it is a simple matter to get the gun on line with the target early in the swinging process and swing down its flight path. After the target passes your barrels you start your swing and shoot right at it while keeping the barrels swinging.

Eye Focal Point

It is important to see the target as soon as possible and track it with your eyes and body. Most shooters don't do enough looking and do too much gun moving. Be a spendthrift with the eyes and a miser with gun movement. When I suggest you be a miser with gun movement I do not mean that you swing slowly or deliberately. What I mean is keep the gun off your shoulder until you are ready to break the target. Don't mount your gun on a long crossing shot and follow it with the barrels. Your swing will slow to a crawl and you will either shoot behind it or try to see a lead the equivalent of 2½ school buses. Watch the targets that you can see for a long time, let the shot develop, then when they pass your barrels in the gun hold point swing through them aggressively and break them. I will discuss some options for long crossing shots later in this chapter.

Experienced shooters realize the advantage of taking a moment to clear the mind and focus the eyes in the area where the target will appear before calling for the target. This should be practiced in all the clay target shooting sports.

Tip: Tracking Targets With Your Eyes: Try this little demonstration that I use in my sporting clays clinics. Select a field with targets that pass through either vegetation or trees. Point your finger up on the target flight path and look out over your finger. With the eyes fixed in position out over your finger, call for a target. Don't move your eyes or attempt to visually track the target, just see it as it passes through your window of vision.

Now, turn your head back and direct your eyes to the very first area where the target is visible as it comes off the machine. Call for the target and focus on it. Swivel your head and track it with your eyes from the moment it is visible until it hits the ground. The second target looked half as fast and twice as big as the first one, didn't it? I'll bet you didn't see any trees or vegetation either, did you? You should look at each and every target with this same degree of intensity and focus. See the target as soon as possible and don't mount the gun until you are ready to break the target.

Tip: Shooting Right At Moving Targets: When I tell a student to shoot right at a target I am actually teaching him to swing through the target. The speed of the swing, which is developed by letting the target pass the muzzles before the gun is mounted, is what provides the forward allowance, or lead. Shooting with this method is a subconscious function. By shooting right at targets in practice or in a clinic, you program the subconscious to break targets. If you try to see a measured lead, which must be determined and calculated on each shot, the conscious mind becomes involved, causing a slower, more deliberate process that is more prone to errors.

How To Shoot Sporting Clays

Crossing Targets

Targets that cross at 90-degree angles require considerable gun speed to overtake and swing through. As a basic rule to increase gun speed, move your gun hold point closer to the machine. It is important to keep most of your weight on the front foot and pivot your body, don't sway.

Fields that feature crossing targets are often named after grouse or woodcock and you will frequently encounter trees and vegetation between you and the target flight path. Remember what I told you earlier about focusing on the target. See it come off the machine, watch it with maximum intensity, and you will never see the trees and other vegetation. Selecting a target break point in an open space and selecting a gun hold point to break it in this opening is how you avoid shooting when a target is behind a four-foot pine tree. If you look at the tree and worry about avoiding it while the target is in flight, you will probably miss both the tree and the target. Don't look at anything you don't want to shoot, and that includes trees, bushes, and gun barrels. Look at the target.

A basic Lincoln trap and the accessories in this photo offer a wide variety of sporting clays targets for practice or some informal shooting at your club. This particular trap and accessories (including my daughter who serves as my trapper) is used at my home in the North Georgian mountains for practicing and field testing shotguns, chokes, and loads. I also take the traps to trap and skeet clubs that don't have a sporting clays course, and use them to teach clinics on combination trap and skeet fields.

It is tempting to check to be sure on a fast-crossing target. Take the advice of a noted British shooting instructor and author, "Swing fast, don't check." I'll add to that my advice, see the ball, not the bat.

Tip: Low-Crossing Targets: Crossing shots that pass down a ravine or those that must be fired down at from a raised platform can be frustrating. The key to breaking these targets is to get plenty of weight out over your front foot, with just the toe of the rear foot touching for balance. Close your stance up so your feet are about the same distance apart as your armpits.

If the target is 20 yards or farther away, I would suggest at least number 8 shot and an improved cylinder choke. The shoulder of a clay target is the most durable part and the hardest place to break a target. When you are shooting down at a target from an angle, I would suggest you tighten up one choke size and increase shot to one size larger. Many people are hitting the often named Chukar targets and not breaking them because of this almost indestructible characteristic of a target struck on the top of the shoulder.

How To Shoot Quartering-Away Targets

Most people miss these targets by mounting the gun and riding them or are fooled into trying to see a lead that is much too long. Watch a good trap shooter break quartering-away targets. He has a high gun hold point out toward the target break point, he lets the shot develop, and when the most important part of making the quartering-away shot occurs, he makes a short, positive stroke, swings through the target and breaks it. Look at how little his gun moves.

If a target is presented to you that is crossing at a 90-degree angle, the gun hold point must be relatively near the trap machine. If it is going almost straight away from you, the gun hold point is out very near the target break point and just below the flight path of the target. Watch the target, let the shot develop, shoot right at the target, and keep the muzzles moving.

Tip: Smoke and String: For the swing-through method to work, the gun barrels must follow the flight path of the target just prior to overtaking the target and during the follow through. If you come from behind a rising target and shoot just as it begins to lose velocity and curve downward, you will shoot over it. If you make a long swing on this target as it climbs upward and shoot just as it begins to curve downward, you will shoot way over it. If you have to shoot a target that is making a drastic change in trajectory, put your gun hold point out near where you will be shooting it. Let it pass your muzzles and shoot it with a short, positive stroke that follows the target flight path. Remember, for swing-through leads to work you must be on the target flight path. As you come up behind the targets, you swing through it and follow through. Most people miss targets because they don't finish the shot and follow-through.

To help you track the exact target flight path, visualize a smoke trail coming out the back of the target. Attach a three foot length of string to a ball and watch how it curves behind the ball as it goes through the air. If you visualize a vapor trail behind your targets and swing your gun up the smoke trail, it may help you learn to follow the target flight path more accurately.

How To Shoot Rabbits

Rabbits are the most unpredictable targets thrown on a sporting clays course. They change speed and direction every time they come in contact with the ground. These changes can be very subtle or extremely drastic. This is also a target on which you cannot procrastinate, deliberate, or anticipate.

Select a target break point at the farthest possible distance you can break the target. You want to select a target break point for a worst-case scenario. Take special care to insure that your gun hold point is below the path of the rabbit. Don't hold high anticipating a bounce. If you get a bounce, it is easy to raise the gun and destroy the target. Don't anticipate specific behavior by the target. Focus on the target and shoot right at it. If you mount your gun and attempt to ride this target across the field, and it has any speed at all, you are giving yourself very little chance to break it.

You must shoot rabbit targets aggressively and with total abandon. Shoot right at it the instant your stock touches your face.

Springing Teal

Most people who have trouble with these vertically launched targets either ride them after the gun is mounted or try to check

This shooter demonstrates excellent form in the ready position for a springing teal target-high gun hold point: weight on the front foot, eyes focused down toward the trap to see the target as soon as it emerges.

and measure leads. Every clay target has two things in common after being launched from a trap machine: They constantly change trajectory and speed. Sometimes these changes in trajectory and speed are obvious, sometimes subtle. Because it is launched almost straight up, the springing teal makes the most drastic changes in both trajectory and speed. When this target comes off the machine it is traveling extremely fast. Just like a space shuttle going into orbit, it requires velocity to overcome gravity. The farther it climbs the more rapidly it slows down. If you mount your gun on this target early in its flight while it is traveling near maximum velocity and shoot it near the top of its flight, you will shoot over it. You shoot high because you initiate your swing on a fast target that is beginning to slow drastically just as you catch it.

It is okay to shoot this target halfway up, but you can't ride it. You must use a low gun hold point and make a big move as soon as you see the target. I suggest you limit your swing to the top third of the target's flight. Your gun hold point should be fairly high, about one-third of the way down from the top of the target's flight to the machine. Visualize if you will that you will execute your swing and break the target in a window that consists of the top one-third of the target's flight. The gun hold point is at the bottom edge of the window. The target will be broken by shooting right at it about half-way up the window. If a pair is thrown, the second target will be broken at the top of this window. Cut your eyes back down to the top of the trap house or wherever the target is first visible. See the target as soon as possible, wait until it flies into the bottom edge of your window, mount the gun as it passes the muzzles and shoot right at it. If shooting a pair, go quickly and directly to the second target and shoot it like it was a chip off the first target.

Tip: Shooting Teal Chips: A good way to learn how to break the second teal when the targets are thrown as a true pair is to shoot singles and then shoot at a fragment from the broken target. This will train you to focus on one target for the first shot and keep your head on your gun for the second.

Shooting Long Crossers

There are three ways to shoot these targets. Some shooters who learn to shoot the swing-through method on a variety of targets at close and medium range have trouble shooting "right at 'em" when the range gets 40 yards or so. The reason swing-through doesn't work for them at extended ranges is that they don't swing, they creep. If you are a swing-through shooter, try this. Pick a gun hold point and mark it with some background feature such as a cloud. Now hold your hand up next to your gun hold point and measure one hand width from your gun hold point. Let the target pass your barrels one hand's width before you make a move to overtake it and swing through. When you do initiate the swing, don't be deliberate, but move aggressively to the target and shoot right at it. You cannot swing too fast on this shot. Just a little slow is too slow.

Another method for shooting long crossers is to use what I call a portable gun hold point. You bring the unmounted gun up behind the target and stay about one hand's width behind it, traveling at about the same speed as the target. As the target approaches the target break point, swing past the target while mounting the gun and shoot right at it. Keep the gun moving.

For those who cannot make either of these methods work on long crossers, I go to my third alternative. This starts off like either of the methods just described, with one exception. You must see a gap—not a measured lead, but a gap—between the target and the barrels. The barrels are swung so this gap continues to expand as the trigger is pulled. Don't look at the barrels: Look at the target, focus on the target. You can see the gap between the target and the gun in your peripheral vision even when you are focused on the target.

Falling Targets

Many shooters have trouble with falling or settling targets. The main reason they miss these targets is that they are deceived into thinking the targets are moving slower than they really are and they try to get under them and see a lead. Using a high gun hold point allows the targets to fall below your barrels, then with a swift deliberate move, mount the gun and shoot right at the target while keeping the gun moving downward. This works just like a target crossing in front of you on a horizontal path. You are still coming from behind the target and swinging through it.

How To Shoot Pairs

The first thing you need to learn about pairs is that there is no such thing, only two singles in flight at the same time. You must focus on the targets one at a time, and you must shoot targets one at a time. If you get lucky and break two targets with one shot in sporting clays, both are counted as dead.

A report pair is when the second target is launched on the sound of the shot fired at the first target. If the targets are coming off the same machine, dismount your gun and swing back to your original gun hold and eye focal points. If you leave your gun mounted and too near your target break point, you have little chance to break the second target. If the targets are launched from two different machines and offer the second target on a separate flight path from the first, dismount your gun after shooting at the first target *and* go to a gun hold point somewhere on the flight path of the second target. Let it pass your barrels, swing through it, shoot at it, and keep those barrels moving.

On a following pair the second target is launched at the discretion of the puller as soon as possible after the first target is launched. These are almost always launched off a single machine. They are called a following pair because the trapper is usually using a manually cocked machine that is too slow for a true report pair. You will have even more time to dismount your gun and return to your gun hold point before this target is launched.

A true pair consists of two targets launched at the same time. They may come off the same trap arm or they may come off two different machines and be flying in opposite directions. In many cases you will not have time to dismount your gun between shots on these targets. If the two targets are launched off the same machine and are traveling in the same direction on similar flight paths, whenever possible take the rear target first, keep the muzzles swinging after the first shot, and break the second. A good way to practice this is to have someone launch single targets and after you break the first target, shoot one of the fragments. This teaches two lessons: Focus on one target and keep your head on the stock. If the gun shifts on your shoulder, it can be quickly remounted with a very short extension of the hand holding the fore-end and raising the stock to your face. This can

For high incomers, many shooters have learned to use a pull-ahead method to obtain the correct forward allowance. Mount the gun slightly behind the target, point just behind the target briefly with the mounted gun, and then swing through the target. As the barrels swing through you'll see just a little daylight. With the gap between target and barrels continuing to expand, pull the trigger. The eyes are intensely focused on the target, with barrels viewed only in the periphery vision and slightly out of focus.

be accomplished quickly and increases your chances of breaking the second target. You have a better chance doing this than trying to break the second target with your face off the stock.

Tip: Seeing One Target: It is critical that you learn to focus on one single target, preferably the rear one, when shooting doubles. If you flick your eyes back and forth you will either slow your swing or shoot directly between them. It is better to break one for sure than miss two because you never decided which one to break.

If a target comes from directly behind you and passes overhead, look straight up to see the target as soon as possible. Let the target pass your barrels. Then, if you swing through the target aggressively, you can break it without seeing any lead. Attack the target and keep the gun moving.

Shooting Overhead Targets

The key to shooting any overhead target is to get your gun hold point up high on the target flight path. Don't set your gun hold point up too close to the machine. Set up pretty close to where you expect to break it, let it pass your muzzles and, using an aggressive swing, catch it and pull the trigger as you pass it— keep the barrels moving.

If you have a target coming from behind you, point your muzzles straight up. When you call for the target, tip your head as far back as you can and roll your eyes back toward the machine. This will enable you to see the target quickly, rather than after it passes over your head and gets way out in front of you, making the shot much more difficult. As the target passes your vertical barrels, point at it with the finger in the fore-end as you mount the gun. Shoot right at it, and keep the gun moving.

Five-Stand Sporting Clays

This is going to be a very popular version of sporting clays, which I predict will equal or exceed the British version in popularity. There are several reasons for my prediction. This layout can be superimposed on skeet-and-trap combination fields, which are already in existence at most gun clubs. Five shooters at a time can shoot the game and no time is lost walking from field to field. This is also the best bet for a sporting clays game in the Olympics because the field can be standardized for competition and practice.

The game is shot from five stands, with one shooter on each stand. On each stand you get a single and two pairs. The combinations of tower, springing teal, left-to-right crosser, right-to-left crosser, rabbit, and incomer afford multiple combinations for

A 5-Stand sporting clays layout is great for practice and instruction. Here, the author works with Casey Adkinson, one of three All-American shooters he coached in 1991. Learning to shoot well is like straightening crooked teeth: you don't straighten crooked teeth with a mallet; you apply gentle pressure over a long period of time. Reaching your peak performance with a shotgun requires the same orthodontic approach—gentle pressure over a long period of time.

singles and doubles on each stand. On each stand you get five targets and then you rotate, as in trap shooting. The National Sporting Clays Association has three of the layouts, which they haul all over the country for demonstrations. I suggest you contact them to schedule a visit to your club.

5-Stand sporting clays is becoming extremely popular because it can be superimposed on an existing trap and skeet layout. The 5-Stand hardware can be quickly moved if you want to use the field for trap or skeet.

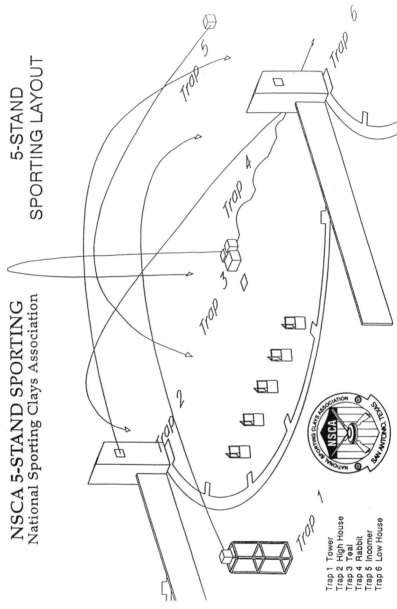

NSCA 5-STAND SPORTING
National Sporting Clays Association

5-STAND
SPORTING LAYOUT

Trap 1
Trap 2
Trap 3
Trap 4
Trap 5
Trap 6

Trap 1 Tower
Trap 2 High House
Trap 3 Teal
Trap 4 Rabbit
Trap 5 Incomer
Trap 6 Low House

For information on obtaining a 5-Stand layout at your club, call 1-800-877-5338.

While awaiting your next shot on 5-Stand, check the menu in your cage and visualize how you will shoot your next pair.

If you have a target launched from a tower and coming from behind you, cut your eyes back toward the tower and view the target as soon as possible. Your gun hold point should be about halfway between where you really see the target clearly and where you intend to break it. *Be a spendthrift with the eyes and a miser with gun movements.* In other words, don't start mounting your gun on a target you haven't seen clearly or read accurately.

International Skeet

Also known as Olympic Skeet, this game is somewhat different than American skeet, which is so popular in the United States. In 1976, due to an increase in higher scores, Olympic skeet rules were changed to make conditions tougher. Again, in January 1990, the Olympic rules committee decided to increase the degree of difficulty by limiting the shot charge to 28 grams or just a little less than 1 ounce.

Course of Fire

Station 1

1 High-House Single

1 Pair of Doubles

Station 2

1 High-House Single

1 Low-House Single

1 Pair

Station 3

1 High-House Single

1 Low-House Single

1 Pair

Station 4

1 High-House Single

1 Low-House Single

Station 5

1 High-House Single

1 Low-House Single

1 Pair Doubles

Station 6

1 High-House Single

1 Low-House Single

1 Pair Doubles

Station 7

1 Pair Doubles

Station 8

1 High-House Single

1 Low-House Single

This course of fire eliminates the "option" shot and the relatively easy singles from stations 1 and 7.

There are some other differences that make International skeet more difficult than its American counterpart. International targets fly from about 59 to 61 yards rather than the 55 yards required by American rules. Each machine has a built-in electronic delay switch that randomly selects and delays launching from 0–3 seconds. After calling for the target, shooters must keep their guns in the ready position, with the toe of the stock below the crest of the hip until the target appears. If you get the long, 3-second delay, it can seem like a lifetime. If you relax at all, in anticipation of a long delay, you may get a target with no delay and never catch up. Letting a high 2 or low 6 get the jump on you has a whole new meaning when you are psyched for a delay and get an instant release. Obviously, the solution to this dilemma is to not think about how long a delay you may get, but simply wait for the target to appear and then go after it with gusto.

A round of registered targets will consist of 200 or 400 targets shot in series of 25 targets. This is another major difference in International and American skeet. In the American version, we shoot four consecutive rounds on the same field with a short break between rounds to get more shells. International skeet targets are shot 25 at a time and then you leave the field and wait until your squad's turn comes up again. Every squad shoots a 25-target round and then waits until every other squad has shot a 25-target round before their turn comes up again. It takes most of a day to shoot 100 International skeet targets. If things are really crowded at a big competition, a 200-target tournament may be scheduled for 50 targets a day for four days.

There is always a shoot-off at International skeet tournaments. At the end of 200 targets, the top six scores shoot a round of 25 and that score is added to their score for the 200 targets for a grand total. The highest grand total wins. If a tie exists, additional 25-target rounds are shot until a winner is determined.

Before you decide you never want to try this game, let's put a few things in perspective. Comparing American to International skeet is like comparing recreational softball to major league baseball. They are different games, shot and developed for different reasons. International skeet has evolved as an Olympic competition in which Olympic champions are determined every four years. While it is the version of skeet most popular in every country except the United States, American skeet is by far the most popular in this country.

Forget about the higher degree of difficulty in International. International skeet is not as readily available to most skeet shooters in the United States. On any given weekend between early spring and late fall, I have more American skeet tournaments within an easy drive of my home in Georgia than International skeet tournaments on the entire East Coast in a whole year.

Hopefully this situation will get better. It is not that difficult for a club to throw International skeet targets, although your trap machines may need some modification to throw targets 60 yards, and you will need to add a delay switch to your trap machines.

You will also need to get some harder International targets to withstand the stress of being thrown a greater distance. If you overcome this little bit of inconvenience, you have another clay target game to shoot at your club. Who knows, a future Olympic shooter may come from your club! The odds are long I admit, but the odds of becoming an Olympic champion are long for any event!

Loads For Shooting Registered Targets

The official rule book for International skeet, available from the NRA, describes International skeet loads as follows: "Before firing, the length of the shell shall not exceed standard specifications of 70 mm. Shot load shall not exceed 28 grams (loading tolerance of 0.5 grams). Pellets shall be spherical in shape, made of lead or lead alloy, and not larger than 2.5 mm diameter (0.1 mm tolerance). Shot may be plated. Any safe powder charge may be used."

Many shooters incorrectly say these are 1-ounce loads, but they are not. They are exactly 0.98756 ounce loads, but when you add the maximum tolerance of 0.5 grams, which equals .017635 ounce, you get 1.005195 ounces. If your load weighs more than this you can be disqualified.

I enclose the following formulas for those of you who wish to calculate ounces to grams and vice versa. To convert grams to ounces, multiply the grams by 0.03527.

EXAMPLE: 28 grams × 0.03527 = 0.098756 ounces.

To convert ounces to grams, divide ounces by 0.03527.

> **EXAMPLE:**   0.98756 ounces divided by 0.03527 = 28.

The difference between a 28-gram load and a 1-ounce load is about five grains. You know how many number 9 high-antimony shot pellets it takes to total five grains? Five or six on my scale. After all the calculations, and after all decimals have been put in the correct location, we are dealing with a total difference between the two loads (1 ounce vs. 28 grams) of about five fewer high-antimony number 9 pellets in a 28-gram load!

I suspect it would be a good idea to have a shot load under the 28-gram-plus-0.5-grams tolerance when you attend a world-class competition. They can get pretty picky about loads at a world-class International skeet tournament.

Loads are limited to any safe powder charge, which usually translates to a 3-dram equivalent load with most experienced shooters, since this is what most of them use.

I would suggest you achieve some degree of proficiency in American skeet before trying the International version. Even if you are very good at American skeet be prepared for a drastic drop in your average. I encourage seasoned American skeet shooters to try this game for several reasons. One is that after shooting several hundred International skeet targets, the American version loses much of its intimidation factor. High 2, low 6, and station 8 targets look downright sluggish after exposure to International speeds and delayed launches.

Guns

Guns for International skeet tend to be a little heavier than for American skeet. The whippy, quick-start and quick-stop characteristics of short-barreled, lightweight guns do not find favor with the International crowd. While it may take a little more punch to get a heavier gun started, you gain in that once you catch up with a fast-flying International target, it is almost impossible to stop it and not follow through. The heavier guns are a little more manageable and more forgiving when traveling at the high speeds required in this game.

International skeet guns, especially those of the top competitors, have stock dimensions closely akin to our American trap stocks. These higher stocks are not to make the guns shoot higher, but to allow a light contact on the face as opposed to having to really get your face down against a low-stocked gun. The high stock helps prevent what Coach Branham calls a "floating head" when there is a slight mismount. Only a slight adjustment is necessary to touch the face to the high stock on a mismount.

Chokes

No real big mystery here. The dimensions of an International skeet field are the same as our American skeet field, so the same chokes ought to suffice, about .005 constrictions. International skeet is the game that spawned the Tula or jug chokes, first used by the Russians. Neophytes at this game or those who shoot it too deliberately may take a little too long on some shots and therefore break targets at slightly longer distances than when shooting American skeet. The differences in where you break American skeet and International skeet should not be great enough to require a change to a tighter choke.

How To Shoot the Game

Ready Position and Gun Mount

When calling for a target, the toe of the stock must be below the crest of the hip. Rules require this be marked with a contrasting

Shawn Dulohery of the United States Army Marksmanship Unit at Fort Benning, Georgia demonstrates the correct ready position and gun mount for International skeet on station one. The white stripe on his vest is required by international rules. The toe of the stock is located more toward the center of his abdomen, rather than directly on the hip. This is perfectly legal and yields a more consistent gun mount than when the stock is actually touching the hip. The rules require the toe to be *below* the crest of the hip not *on* the crest of the hip—a mistake for new International skeet shooters.

line on your outer shooting garment. The mark must reach from your hip to the front of your vest. The gun may not be raised until the target is visible.

This extremely low ready position can mess with your mind if you let it. Too often new shooters in this game worry about getting the gun up to their face in time to break the target. I quote Coach Burl Branham of the Army Marksmanship Unit: "No one has ever forgotten to mount their gun. A lot of shooters have forgotten to swing!" The gun will come to your face with a little practice.

Don't try to mount the gun and then swing after the target. The first move, as soon as the target is seen, is along the line of flight. The gun is brought to your face as you are swinging with the target, not as a separate and distinct motion.

The wrist of the hand that holds the grip should be cocked. This will greatly increase speed and control when mounting the gun.

Extending the finger on the hand holding the fore-end and using it to point at targets works well in International skeet, as demonstrated by Todd Graves of the United States Army Marksmanship Unit and member of both the 1992 olympic trap and skeet teams. Note Todd's classic form, with his nose directly over the toes of his front foot.

Tip: Bend Both Knees: To insure that you swing with your whole body rather than swaying or swinging with just your arms, slightly bend both knees.

Leads

A champion International skeet shooter must be able to break any target on the field with a sustained lead, a pull-ahead, or a swing-through lead. In most cases the shooter tries to see a sustained lead, but if things go awry, he must use one of the others. As an example, a good shooter might break a high 2 well before the center stake and the next time break it well past the center stake. You rarely see the machine-like precision of American skeet breaking the targets in the same spot every time. A good International shooter must be adaptable.

It surprises many American skeet shooters when they discover that the sustained leads they used in American skeet are very close to those required for International. The International gets are flying faster, but your gun swing is also moving faster. The major exceptions are incomers on 1, 2, 6, and 7. It is easy for a skeet shooter who has shot a lot of the American version to shoot way behind these targets. That is the voice of experience talking.

Tip: Leads Are a Subconscious Function: In preparation for this book I made several trips to the Army Marksmanship Unit at Ft. Benning, since this facility has produced many of our Olympic, National, and Pan American International Skeet shooters, including the likes of Dan Carlisle and Mat Dryke. In one of the many sessions I had with Coach Branham, he explained how lead is determined in International skeet.

"International skeet is a subconscious game. The subconscious knows no true or false. If you put in bad information, that is what comes out. It is very hard to get bad information out of the subconscious once it has been implanted. Only perfect practice makes perfect."

Those five sentences sum up the basic philosophy of a man who is the Vince Lombardi of International skeet and trap shooting coaches.

Station 1—High House

High Single: Stations 1 and 8 are the only two on the field where you can do a practice mount or sight your shotgun before calling for the target. The gun must be dismounted prior to calling for the target.

The gun hold point is directly over the center stake on the target flight line. Look up above the barrels to see the target. This target needs to be floated about six inches above the barrels.

Focus on the target: Don't look at the muzzles. See the target! Don't be spooked by the sound of the machine. Don't measure and ride this one. The gun goes off when the stock touches the cheek.

The ready position for station 1. Eyes are looking up over the barrels.

Too much force with your right hand during mounting can cause your muzzles to "seesaw" and make you shoot under this target. Remember: smooth, controlled mount, and shoot when the stock touches your face. Extend the forefinger of your left hand and point at the target as you mount. On this and all targets you should be consciously pointing the barrels at the target during the mount; otherwise you will end up with a beautifully executed mount pointing at absolutely nothing—and that is probably what you will hit!

Station 1—Doubles

Shoot the high house just like a single, just before it reaches the center stake. As soon as the first shot is taken, cut your eyes to the second target and swing through it, seeing about one-and-one-half feet of lead. Keep the gun moving. It is easy to slow your gun down and shoot behind this one. Keep your weight on the front foot (about 60/40) and pivot your whole body.

Todd Graves waits for high one to come out over his head. His eyes are turned up to see the target early but his head is in position for the stock to come to his face on the mount.

Ready position for high 2. Gun muzzles are pointed up toward the target flight path.

Station 2—High House

Feet should be shoulder-width apart and positioned so your belt buckle is pointed to the right-front half of the station pad. Gun hold point is just past parallel with the face of the trap house. Eye focal point is the target opening. Some shooters have to turn their heads back toward the house to clearly see this target come out. This is okay and better than seeing it too late. The first move upon seeing the target exit is with the left pushing the barrels to the right along the target flight path. The lead on this one can be anywhere from the front edge to one-and-one-half feet, depending on which method of forward allowance you were forced to use and where you caught the target.

Be ready when you call for this target and start moving the muzzles the instant it appears. Do not try to make sure on this target, nor do you want to rush it.

Station 2—Low House

Foot position is the same and the gun hold point is halfway between the center stake and the low house, with the barrels just

World record holder Bill Roy demonstrates the classic ready position for high 2, with gun hold point up towards the target flight path and eyes focused just outside the target opening.

Ready position for low 2.

under the target flight line. Start the barrels smoothly as the target emerges. How much lead you see depends on whether you shoot it at the crossing stake or closer to the high house. Indifference causes more lost targets here than anything else. This is an easy target, unless you miss it! See your lead and keep the gun moving.

Station 2—Doubles

Shoot the high house just like the single. As soon as the high house breaks, cut your eyes to the left of your barrels, taking care to keep your face against the stock, swing through the incoming low house, and break it. The lead will be a little less than when you shot the single with sustained lead. Keep the gun moving and your head down.

Station 3—High House

The middle stations of 3, 4, and 5 are the ones where mastering the sustained lead helps tame International targets. You must still be prepared to salvage a lost target with the swing-through method if one of the middle stations gets away from you.

Ready position for high 3.

The gun hold point should be about two-thirds of the way back from the center stake to the high house and just below the bottom of the target opening. The eye focal point is just to the right of the target opening. If this target is constantly jumping you, move your barrels out away from the house slightly. If you get out too far, you won't have any trouble getting in front of high 3, but your muzzles will be moving too slow for your leads to work. Gun hold points on all the middle stations are critical and it is worth some of your practice time to experiment and find out what is best for you.

Keep your weight over the front foot, and pivot, don't sway. Concentrate and be ready—really ready—when you call for this target.

Station 3—Low House

This target, along with high 5, requires the longest lead in skeet. Your gun hold point is about two-thirds of the way back from the center stake to the low house. This target is climbing from the moment it is launched. Many people miss it because they start off with their barrels too high and swing straight across the field at the same level, and as the target continues to rise they shoot

Ready position for low 3.

under it. Make sure your gun hold point is on the target flight line on all middle-station low-house targets.

Keep your weight over your front foot and your head down. Stopping the gun is a common error on this target. Keep the gun moving.

Station 3—Doubles

Shoot the high house just like the single and see it break. Cut your eyes to the low-house target, being careful to keep your head on the stock. Swing through it and use the pull-away lead method. The pull-away lead is achieved by swinging through the target and seeing some daylight open up between the barrels and the target. Keep moving your barrels so that this opening appears to be getting larger and pull the trigger. This patch of daylight doesn't have to be very wide, but it is important that it continue to expand as you fire.

Keep your weight over the front foot and your head down. Don't rush the high house because you are worried about the low-house target. There is no such thing as doubles, just two singles in the air at the same time. That is how you must think of them and that is how you must break them.

Station 4—High House

With no doubles on this station, many shooters tend to become a little too casual and drop targets they should have broken. Maintain your aggression and attack these targets. Break them near the center stake. The gun hold point for this one is somewhere between two-thirds and halfway back to the high house from the center stake. If you are fast and have good reflexes, you will favor the two-thirds-of-the-way-back hold point. The rest of us will have to move out closer to the halfway mark. It is not advisable to come any closer than halfway from the high house to the center stake. If your gun hold point gets too close to the center stake, your muzzles will lack the speed necessary to make your leads work.

Look just to the right of the target opening and start swinging your muzzles as soon as the target appears. Don't ride this target. When the lead is right, shoot it and follow through. Break this one as near the center stake as possible.

Ready position for high 4.

Ready position for low 4.

Station 4—Low House

This one is a mirror image of the high house technically, but there are some mental adjustments that must be made. Low 4 is the first fast low-house target seen in a round of skeet. Up until now, the low has been an incomer viewed from a distance, allowing all sorts of time to establish leads and barrel alignment. Your gun hold point is about one-half to two-thirds of the way back from the center stake to the low house. It is a mistake to shoot the high house and then quickly turn to your right and call for the low house. Take a second in between these two targets and get your mind focused on the low-house target. Be ready for this target and start swinging your barrels the moment it appears.

This is also the first station where a poor background may begin to interfere with your ability to see the target. Move your eye focal point out just a little if you are having trouble seeing this target.

Station 5—High House

This is the most frequently missed incomer on the skeet field. Many people like to wait and take this target when it is almost two-thirds of the way from the center stake to the low house. This is a mistake, because by then the target has lost velocity, is susceptible to wind, and is beginning to drop. A head wind can also drastically reduce the speed of this target and the lead it takes to break it.

The gun hold point is halfway between the center stake and the high house and just below the target's line of flight. Break this one right over or just after it crosses the center stake. To ride it is to court disaster.

Remember, this target and low 3 require the longest leads on the skeet field. When the lead is correct, shoot, keep your head down, and the gun moving.

Station Five—Low House

This is one of the most missed targets in both American and International skeet. Cluttered background, a target that appears to be traveling very fast, and a target that is climbing are all factors that contribute to the extreme difficulty of this target.

The gun hold point is halfway between the center stake and the low house. As you shoot this target a bit and it becomes a little easier, you may want to move your gun hold in a little closer to the low house.

Be sure your barrels are below the target flight path and swing along the flight path. Remember that this target is still climbing when you break it just before or right over the center stake. Try to avoid shooting it any later if you can possibly do so. If it gets away from you, then you will have to swing through it out past the center stake, which is risky.

Station 5—Doubles

To facilitate the performance of a good follow through on the high-house target, I suggest you right-hand shooters set your foot position so a line drawn across your toes is parallel to the right side of this station's pad. This is also the recommended foot position for the high-house single on this station.

It is imperative that you keep your weight over the front foot and pivot your whole body on these two shots. Shoot the low house just like the single, see it break, then cut your eyes to the right of your barrels to pick up the incoming high-house target. Swing aggressively through the high-house target and keep your barrels moving. If you find yourself constantly shooting behind this target with a swing-through lead, use the pull-away lead, where you are conscious of the lead constantly expanding as you shoot.

Ready position for high 6.

Ready position for low 6.

Station 6—High House

This is the easiest target you will have had since the station 2 low house. Don't let it lull you into mental complacency. Avoid the temptation to ride it. The gun hold point should be halfway between the center stake and the high house. Break it just after it crosses the center stake.

Station 6—Low House

Like high 2, this target presents an optical illusion. It whizzes past you looking like it is traveling twice as fast as anything else on the field. Don't let it fool you. You can counter a lot of this target's illusion of speed by moving your gun hold point out a little past parallel to the face of the trap house, starting your swing the instant you see it appear in the target opening, and shooting it with a swing-through lead. You may need to experiment with just how far past parallel you need to hold your barrels.

Another common error here is that the shooter will have his barrels too high and the target will actually go under the barrels. Parallel to the ground is just about as high as you should go with your gun hold point here. If you get a false start on this target, you will never recover. See it emerge and start your swing instantly.

Station 6—Doubles

Shoot the low house just like the single. Don't rush it. After you see the low house break, cut your eyes to the right of your barrels and see the high-house incomer. Keep your head on the stock. because it is very easy for a right-handed shooter to pull the gun away from the face on the second target. Using the arms instead of pivoting the entire body is easy to do on this second target, and that is what pulls the gun away from your face.

After all the middle stations and the fast, outgoing low-house target, the incomer looks very slow. It isn't! Be aggressive and follow through.

Station 7—Doubles

There ought to be a neon sign that lights up every time we step onto station 7 that says, "There are no easy ones!" Complacency causes more misses here than all the possible errors in technique

Ready position for station 7.

combined. Don't "showboat" and shoot the low-house target five feet in front of your muzzles. Look at the low house—really look at it—and break it just before the center stake. See it break. The high-house incomer should be just passing your barrels or slightly to the right as you break low six. Use an aggressive swing-through lead and keep the gun moving. If you shoot the low house too quickly, your barrels will be too far out in front of the incomer and you will be in big trouble. If you catch yourself in this unhappy situation, start moving your muzzles immediately and shoot it with a sustained lead, seeing about a one-and-one-half foot lead. Keep your head down and those barrels moving for a good follow through.

Station 8—High House

This is the only station other than station 1 on which you can mount your gun and take a practice point before calling for the target. I suggest you take advantage of this privilege. Position

Ready position for high 8. The shooter has positioned himself on the back corner of the pad and to the far left of the pad. This prevents the shooter from being "jammed" by a target that comes inside the crossing stake.

your feet so you can point your barrels about fifteen feet high, directly over the crossing stake. Swing your barrels back to the gun hold point, which is about three feet to the right and level with the bottom right-hand corner of the target opening. Dismount your gun to the ready position and call for the target. As soon as it appears in the target opening, start your swing and shoot right at it. Your gun will be moving so fast that by the time you catch it, you will attain the correct lead.

Station 8—Low House

Set up with your mounted gun pointed fifteen feet over the center stake and pivot your whole body back to your gun hold point, about a yard above the upper right-hand corner of the target opening and a yard to the right of the edge of the trap house. Dismount your gun to the ready position and call for the target. The instant you see it emerge from the target opening, start your swing and shoot right at it.

If you are having problems with either or both targets on station 8, back off the station about ten yards and shoot them until you are breaking them consistently. Gradually move closer to the station until you are back on the pad. This exercise takes a lot of the intimidation out of this target.

Tip: See the Target, Start Swing Immediately: You must be mentally and physically ready for this target when you call for it. If you start your swing too early before it comes out, you are in trouble. If you delay your swing, you are in trouble. See the target, and start instantly.

I asked Coach Branham why he thought International skeet was not very popular in this country. "International skeet is a hard game. The NSSA shooters don't want to take a drop in scores down to the 70s and 80s. About the only thing you can win are medals and some NRA award points. Those who have the money don't have the time to master the game. Those who have the time don't have the money."

Joe Morales demonstrates perfect form in keeping his head on the stock during and after the shot. The ejected empty is in the air and Joe still has his head firmly planted on the stock in this International skeet tournament.

International Skeet Shoots

For information on International skeet shoots contact the National Skeet Shooting Association or the National Rifle Association at the addresses listed in the appendix.

International Trap

International trap is often called bunker trap, trench, Olympic trap or International clay pigeon. In my opinion this is the hardest clay target game to master of all the games shot on standard regulation fields. This is not a game for tyro shotgunners. Even shooters with several years' experience at American trap will suffer severe ego damage when they first attempt International trap. But that's no big deal since most of us usually start with low scores and work our way up in just about any new clay target shooting sport we try.

There are over half a million registered shooters in Italy, almost all of whom shoot international trap exclusively. They have over 300 international trap fields; there are twelve to fourteen in the USA.

There are some major differences in American trap and International trap. In the International version, targets are thrown farther, at varying degrees in elevation, and at more extreme angles than in American trap. The targets are also harder than those used in American trap because of the increased distances they are thrown. Loads are limited to 28 grams, which calculates to just under 1

This explains why International trap is often called "bunker trap": all fifteen machines are below ground in a bunker.

The first three trap machines in this photo all throw targets for post one. A computer randomly selects which of the three will launch the target.

ounce. That's the bad news. The good news is you get two shots at each target and breaking a target with the second shot counts just as much as one broken on the first shot.

Unlike American trap—in which a single trap machine is placed 16 yards in front of an arch-shaped, 5-station field—International trap uses 15 machines located in an underground bunker 16½ yards in front of five shooting stations. There are three traps in front of each station, each set to throw targets at various angles and elevations. In addition to wider lateral angles and greater variations in vertical angles, International targets are thrown 50 percent farther than targets used in the American version.

How the Game Is Shot

International trap squads consist of six shooters. Five of the members are spread out, one at each of the five stations, with the sixth shooter standing behind the shooter on station 1. After the shooter on station 1 calls for his target and shoots it, the sixth squad member comes up and stands to his left. After the shooter on station 2 shoots, the shooter who started on station 1 moves over to occupy station 2. This shifting continues across the field. When the shooter on station 5 shoots his target, he turns to the right and walks around behind the squad to station 1. To a new shooter this is a lot like shooting on a merry-go-round and will seem quite strange at first. After a few rounds you will feel comfortable with the constant moving.

This game is shot totally with the subconscious mind. Calculations and deliberation will only breed low scores.

I asked Coach Branham what it took to be a good International trap shooter. Without hesitation or qualification, he answered with one word, "Determination!" I must concur. Unlike some disciplines where specific leads, gun hold points, and target break points can be customized for each shooter and then memorized, International trap requires each and every target be broken using a swing-through/instinctive technique implanted in the subconscious. The only way to accomplish this is to shoot a tremendous number of International trap targets. If you spend a lot of time looking at International trap targets and going through mental calisthenics to determine how much lead you should see on a specific target, you won't break many.

As in all clay shooting disciplines, there some basic shooting techniques that will encourage good form and allow you to improve your skill level. Since each shooting station has its own group of three trap machines, for all practical purposes the physical layout of every station is identical. Unlike American trap, where the angles to the trap house differ, requiring different hold points, International targets are shot using the same technique on every station. About the only exception to this is when a particular station has some sort of unusual background feature that may require a slight modification in gun hold point and eye focal point.

Foot Position

Since you don't know which trap the target will come from or the angle and elevation it will take, about the best you can do with foot position is to set up right in the middle of the station. Due to personal difficulties with certain targets, everyone will not use exactly the same foot position. A good starting place is with the front foot pointed directly at the stripe on the trap house just over the center trap for your station. The best shooters in this game use a rather narrow stance, with their feet almost directly under the armpits.

Stance

Unlike international skeet where you see some rather unorthodox stances, the best International trap shooters use an erect stance and swing primarily from the waist up. I have mentioned upper body integrity in several other places in this book, but it bears mention again. The upper body must function like the turret on a military tank. Attempting to shoot International trap targets with excessive arm swing is an exercise in frustration.

Gun Mount

To avoid being too hunched over, most international trap shooters mount the gun at a fairly high angle and then lower the barrels to the gun hold point.

Gun Hold Point

The vast majority of the really good international trap shooters point directly at the stripe on the trap house roof in front of their shooting station. This allows them to get onto the target flight line quickly with their muzzles and swing through the target. The better International trap shooters appear to take the targets much quicker than the garden-variety shooters. I suspect this is in part

The white stripe in the center of this photo marks the location of the center trap machine in this International trap bunker. The mark is used by International trap shooters as a reference point for their gun hold point prior to calling for a target. Most shooters hold their muzzles over this stripe near the front edge of the trap house.

due to good visual skills, but primarily because they use a low gun hold point and start moving the gun instantly along the line of flight as soon as the target appears.

A new shooter may want to hold slightly above the front edge of the bunker. This may create a few problems with low targets, but it may help you catch up with most of the others while learning the game. A one-eyed shooter has no choice. He must have his barrels below the edge of the bunker or his barrels will obscure all straight-aways coming out of the center machine.

Eye Focal Point

A common error with novice International trap shooters occurs when they become intimidated by the speed of the targets coming off the trap machine, and in an attempt to see the target quicker they focus closer and closer to the front edge of the trap house. This actually makes the target appear to be even faster and more difficult to focus on and read quickly. If you look too closely at the house in this game, all you will see is a blur as the target is launched. Look a few yards in front of the trap house so you will be able to see the target clearly and not have to refocus your eyes while tracking a blurred streak. It will take a little experimentation to determine just how far out you need to focus. As a rule of thumb, if you are having trouble seeing International trap targets, move your eye focal point slightly away from the house rather than closer to it.

As your level of competence increases, you can experiment with bringing your eye focal point back toward the edge of the bunker.

The eyes should be on wide-angle focus. Tunnel vision will make these targets difficult to see and almost impossible to track.

Leads

The only feasible system of leading these fast, unpredictable targets is with the swing-through method. These targets are so fast and get so far ahead of the barrels of even shooters with exceptional hand speed, very little if any lead needs to be seen. By the time you catch up with these targets, your muzzles are really moving. Some shooters do try to see a little daylight on the extreme left and right angles, but only a gap and not a specific measured lead.

Guns, Loads, and Chokes

Due to the extreme variations in elevation, guns for International trap shooting are not stocked as high as those used for American trap, where all targets are rising at a consistent angle. An international trap target launched at a much steeper angle than American trap may be followed by one much lower than an American trap target and may never rise above the level of the station you are standing on. A gun stocked to shoot high would require a great deal of daylight between the barrels and one of these low-flying targets.

I don't recall ever having seen anything but a 12 gauge on an International trap field. The game is hard enough without handicapping yourself with a small-gauge shotgun. Over-and-unders dominate this game. I suspect this is due to the shooter being allowed two shots. If a second shot is required, the advantage of a tight choke is desirable. Most top shooters in this game shoot 3 dram equivalent, high-antimony 8s through improved-modified chokes in the first barrel. Experienced shooters usually take this first shot at somewhere between 33 and 38 yards. For that second shot, usually taken at about 40 to 48 yards, the most popular combination is 3¼-dram equivalent, plated 7½s fired through full chokes.

Tips:

It is a good idea to indulge in a few practice sessions early in your career. If you have a club near you with an International trap field, try to arrange to shoot when they are not so busy, so you can work on specific aspects of the game.

Practice and Training

Although two shots are allowed at each target, I suggest new shooters only load one shell. This will cause you to focus on your first shot and concentrate on reading the target and breaking it. I don't recommend any inexperienced shooter learning a new game start off by shooting two shots at every target. Some advanced shooters take two shots at all targets in practice. Even if they break a target with the first shot, they shoot the biggest piece with the second barrel. There are some respected shooting coaches who do not train with this two-shots-on-every-target philosophy. Instead, they use training sessions that concentrate on breaking the target with the first shot. Many experienced shooters and coaches agree that you must break at least 75 percent of your targets with the first barrel to be competitive.

One exception is for those shooters who want to take their head off the stock after the first shot. Taking a second shot at every target will help them learn to keep their heads down and "stay in their guns."

Another exercise that will help you attain a higher skill level early in your International trap career is to practice shooting the same target for ten or twelve shots. Start off with a straight-away and then go on to targets with various angles and elevations. Be sure to shoot all of the extreme angles and elevations in your early practices and you will see that they can be broken and you will be less intimidated by them. If you shoot ten or twelve low targets in succession, they won't look as tough as when a maximum low target comes right behind one that was at maximum elevation. If you schedule practice during times when the club is not busy, you can have the trapper throw any targets you need to practice on.

As your level of expertise increases you should begin to work on your second-shot technique. Now is the time to take a second shot at every target and shoot at a piece when you break it on the first shot.

International trap fields are expensive to build and any degree of success at this game requires a lot of dedication and practice. But I think it is the most challenging of all the clay target games and the most difficult to shoot well.

If you would like to try International trap, you may have a little difficulty finding a place to shoot. I suggest you contact the National Rifle Association, National Shooting Sports Foundation or the Pacific International Trap Association for locations nearest you. All are listed in the appendix at the end of this book.

I suggest you consult a current rule book for any changes in International trap rules and reputations. They are subject to occasional change.

The Mental Aspects of Shooting

The most critical aspect of mastering any clay target game is mental. One of the most frequently repeated cliches on any clay target field is: "It's 95 percent mental and 5 percent physical." Skeet shooters say it, trap shooters say it, and sporting clays shooters say it. Yet most garden variety shooters only practice the physical aspects of the game and seldom, if ever, practice the mental portion of the game.

We never accomplish anything or achieve anything worthwhile without first visualizing that achievement. You don't suddenly graduate from high school or college. First you see it in your mind as a goal you want to achieve and then you work toward achieving it. First you want it to happen, then you expect it to happen, and then you make it happen.

All major achievements begin with a dream, like breaking 25 straight in your favorite clay target game, or moving up a class, or becoming an AA shooter, or winning some big tournament. Dream is another word for goal.

**Outstanding skeet and trap sporting clays shooter
Dan Mitchell spends a good deal of his practice
time working on the mental game. When you
reach his advanced skill level, the physical moves
are pretty well mastered.**

Daydreaming is nothing more than visualizing goals we want to achieve. Unfortunately, too many potentially great shooters stop at the daydreaming stage without putting into action the rest of the mental process that produces the realization of your personal goals. A dream becomes a goal when you put it on paper and then make a schedule to make it happen.

One of the first steps in achieving your personal goals requires about an hour in a quiet place, a sheet of typing paper, and a pencil. In the middle of the paper write down a goal you want to achieve. It may be to break 100 straight, or compete in a state, zone, national, or international tournament, or become a class AA shooter. Draw a circle around that goal and write down all the reasons why you would enjoy achieving that goal. Let your mind run free and think of all the benefits you would derive from fulfilling this dream. Write them all down, draw a circle around them, and connect them with a line to your original goal in the middle of the page. A new shooter may have a sheet very similar to the example provided. After you have completed this exercise, put the paper away. In a few days get out a new sheet and repeat the exercise without looking at the first sheet. After completing the second sheet, compare it with the first one. You will probably discover you have thought of some additional benefits and experiences associated with your goal. Combine all the rewards and benefits onto one sheet and put it away.

Over the next few days, spend some time daydreaming about your goal. You can daydream while stuck in traffic, waiting for an appointment, when you first wake up in the morning before you get out of bed, or at night before falling asleep.

Daydreaming reinforces your determination to achieve your goal. If you don't want something you won't work for it. The more you dream about something and fantasize about obtaining it, the harder you will work for it. Don't worry about failing or all the hard work it will take to achieve your goal. Think about the pleasure you will experience when you achieve your goal.

After two or three sessions with pencil and paper, it is time to write your plan. This should also be done in writing and contain specific goals and dates. Let's suppose you are a fairly new shooter and want to compete in a major competition that is a year away. What would you do first?

You might want to consider participating in a shooting clinic at a nearby club. Taking lessons from a certified instructor might be a wise move early in your career.

Set up a training schedule with specific dates and goals. The following is an example of a training schedule for a novice skeet shooter. We will assume he can afford to shoot 200 targets a week on Wednesday nights after work and on the weekend.

WEEK ONE

WEDNESDAY NIGHT

FIRST 25

SHOOT REGULAR ROUND FOR SCORE

SECOND 25

FIVE SHOTS ON HIGH 6

FIVE SHOTS ON HIGH 2

FIVE SHOTS ON HIGH 7

FIVE SHOTS ON LOW 4

FIVE SHOTS ON HIGH 4

THIRD 25

STATION ONE – 1 HIGH HOUSE, 2 PAIR DOUBLES

STATION TWO – 2 HIGH HOUSES, 1 PAIR DOUBLES

STATION THREE – 2 HIGH HOUSES, 2 LOW HOUSES

STATION FOUR – 2 HIGH HOUSES, 2 LOW HOUSES

STATION FIVE – 2 HIGH HOUSES, 2 LOW HOUSES

STATION SIX – 2 LOW HOUSES, 1 PAIR DOUBLES

FOURTH 25

REGULAR ROUND FOR SCORE

SATURDAY AFTERNOON

FIRST 25

SHOOT FOR SCORE

SECOND 25

FIVE SHOTS EACH ON FIVE MOST MISSED TARGETS LAST PRACTICE

THIRD 25

REPEAT FIVE SHOTS EACH ON FIVE MOST MISSED TARGETS LAST PRACTICE

FOURTH 25

SHOOT FOR SCORE

Similar schedules can be designed and implemented until you achieve a specific measurable goal. If you reach a plateau and can't seem to continue improving, get some help.

Visualization

The skill of visualization, like any other acquired skill, doesn't happen overnight. It takes practice. Visualization is nothing more than assuming a relaxed state and imagining yourself performing a specific task correctly. I suggest you get a copy of Dr. Charles A. Garfield's book, *Peak Performance.* It outlines the visualization process in detail.

I have addressed visual focus many times in this book in reference to breaking targets. You must also learn to focus mentally on the task at hand, breaking one target at a time.

Here are some suggestions on how to focus mentally on breaking targets. Let's assume you are shooting in a tournament. Mental focus begins before you ever get out of bed.

When you first wake up and realize that today you will be shooting in a tournament, focus your thoughts on shooting well. Don't allow your thoughts to drift to subjects like the specific targets you missed last tournament or in practice. Visualize yourself grinding those targets into dust. Don't allow thoughts of other competitors who may be shooting. You can't shoot them, you can shoot targets, so let your thoughts be occupied with breaking targets. See them break in your mind.

Get to the field early. Visit with your friends, relax and become acclimated to the atmosphere of the tournament. If there is a practice field available, shoot a warm-up round to loosen up. Don't count missed or broken targets. This is like a baseball player taking batting practice before a game. Basketball players warm up by taking shots at the basket. Do you think they keep score during their warm-up? Quarterbacks throw passes before a game to loosen up. Are they counting completed passes? A warm-up round is just that—warm-up.

Get to the field where you are scheduled to shoot. Watch the squad ahead of you, and observe the targets. Don't watch the shooters; look at the targets. Note if the targets are flying high, low, or are affected by the wind. Don't view any of this as negative information. If the targets are unusual, just knowing that gives you an advantage over the shooter who doesn't notice until he has dropped a few targets.

When you step up and call for that first target, erase everything from your mind except breaking this one target. Some shooters tense up before the first target. The first one is no more or less important than all the rest.

Load your gun, position yourself to break the target, assume your ready position, take a deep breath, visualize the technique for breaking this one target as you have done so many times in practice, and see the target break in your mind.

Focus on your eye focal point, look for the target, and be ready mentally and physically. Now let your mind go blank and call for the target. See the target and react to it.

All mental deliberation must take place before you call for the target. This will allow you to shoot in a subconscious state. It

Shooting instructor Tom Sebring visualizes blowing a springing teal target to dust at the NSCA National Championships.

In addition to avidly practicing visualization, Bill Roy also has a unique mental routine he performs before each shot. He selects some feature in the ground in front of the shooting station, such as a blade of grass, a pebble, or something similar, and points his gun at it. His theory is that he is preparing his mind, eyes, and hands to work together and point instinctively at a target. It must work because he holds an International skeet world record.

Focus on the target and nothing else. If you focus visually and mentally on just one target and nothing else you will probably break it. If you are distracted by anything, you will most surely miss. The airplane in the upper left-hand corner could be a distraction and the other target is perhaps even more tempting. Don't look at the second target until the first is broken.

will take some practice to develop your mental game, but in the long run it will be one of your greatest assets.

If you miss a target, forget it. It is gone. You can't birdie the next station and get it back. What you must do is not to keep playing the miss over and over in your mind and use positive visualization to help you hit another one. This is a difficult thing to do, but do it you must or one miss will multiply itself many times before the round is over.

Don't count targets as you shoot. You can look at the score board later. The best way in the world to shoot a 99, 98, or something worse is to think about running a 100 straight about halfway through a round without having dropped a target. Every 100 straight ever recorded was shot one target at a time.

Competitions, do not consist of target events—they consist of one hundred one-target events. That is a play on words, but that is how you must focus on targets—not one hundred at a time, not twenty five, not even the other target in doubles, but one at a time. The only target that matters is the one you are shooting at right now. *Photo:* Jennifer Maier

Clay Target Competition

If you shoot clay targets long enough, sooner or later you will begin to wonder how well you would do in competition. If you have ever considered shooting in competition, I urge you to "Give it a go," as my British shooting friends say. Tournaments come in many different formats. Do not assume competition includes only shooting registered targets, competing in the Grand American Trap Shoot, the NSSA World Skeet Shooting Championships, or the Olympics.

Many gun clubs hold tournaments and throw unregistered targets. At the end of the year, winners in each class are recognized and presented trophies. One of the most practical prizes I have seen awarded at a small club tournament was a bag of shot to the winner in each class and to the guy who finished last. I always felt like the guy who finished last should have gotten two bags because he needed the most practice.

Many clubs have shooting leagues in one or more clay target games. Most clubs near large metropolitan areas have evening leagues that shoot under lights. These evening leagues are excellent training opportunities for aspiring tournament shooters. They provide regular matches in which you shoot for score. Plus you learn to shoot under lights, which is a completely different situation than shooting in daylight, and will provide valuable experience, since most ties are broken by shoot-offs under lights.

Dan Mitchell at Wolf Creek Gun Club in Atlanta, Georgia, runs a very popular clay target league called "The Wednesday Night League." Do they shoot trap, skeet or sporting clays, you might wonder? The answer is—yes. They shoot a different clay game every night. It might be 16-yard trap one week, skeet the next, followed by sporting clays, then handicap trap, then skeet doubles.

Another advantage for a new shooter in a league is the opportunity to chart misses and find out which targets require priority in practice. League shooting combined with regular practice and lessons from a qualified instructor will produce significant improvement in a new shooter or even a more experienced shotgunner who only shoots a round or two on an irregular basis.

Some leagues are affiliated with one of the national clay target associations and offer exceptional prizes. One of the shooters in our NSSA skeet league at Wolf Creek won a new Buick. You don't have to shoot the highest score to win prizes in these nationwide leagues. All you have to do is shoot the required minimum number of targets and your name goes into the pot for a random drawing for guns, ammo, and other gear.

A current trend in tournaments is collectively known as "fun shoots." These are trap, skeet or sporting clays tournaments open to club members and nonmembers alike. Many clubs use these events to recruit new members. One of the best ways to get new shooters to try your club is to set up a two-man tournament that consists of one club member and one non-club member. A five-man team-club tournament could work the same way—one member recruits four non-members for his team.

Fund-raisers for local charities usually throw unregistered targets, with proceeds going to some local worthy cause. In addi-

Many youngsters miss shooting competitions because their parents don't realize that most major tournaments have junior and sub-junior classifications. If we are to attract the next generation of shooters, all tournament organizers must realize the importance of including concurrent classifications for junior shooters.

tion to being a lot of fun, this type of tournament generates favorable publicity for gun owners.

National conservation organizations like Ducks Unlimited and Quail Unlimited put on some fantastic tournaments with unbelievable prizes. These groups put on local, state, and national shoots that are well organized and loads of fun. These tournaments, especially at the state and national level, will usually include more than one clay target game. At the big Ducks Unlimited shoots, you shoot trap, skeet, sporting clays, or a combination of trap or skeet and sporting clays.

If you lean toward more serious competition you may want to consider participating in registered tournaments. When a tournament is registered it simply means it is sanctioned by one of the clay target shooting organizations such as The Amateur Trap Shooting Association, National Skeet Shooting Association, National Sporting Clays Association, or the National Rifle Association. You must be a member of the sanctioning organization to shoot registered targets.

Learn to relax when you are not shooting. The time to be intense and focused is when the target is in the air. Pacing and fretting between rounds expends physical and mental energy that will serve better when the targets are in the air. *Photo:* **Jennifer Maier**

There are many small registered tournaments held every weekend. To find one near you, contact the nearest club or one of the organizations listed in the back of this book. They will provide information and a shoot schedule.

Shooters in these tournaments earn classifications based on their average score. This allows new shooters to have a chance to win their "class" by shooting against other shooters of like ability. When you begin shooting registered targets you won't have a classification so you will usually shoot in "non-classified" against other non-classified shooters.

In most organizations you will receive your classification after shooting your first 300 targets and you will be reclassified at regular intervals thereafter. Subsequently you can go to the Grand American, the World Skeet Shooting Championships, or the National Sporting Clays Championships and compete against other shooters in your class with comparable ability.

If you stay with it long enough, you may someday be selected as a member of an All-American Team or win a state, national, or world championship. No matter what level of achievement you aspire to, shooting in competition can be one of the most exciting things you can do with a shotgun. If you have been shooting trap, skeet, or sporting clays for a few months and really enjoy the game, I urge you to enter a tournament—you won't be sorry.

Tips For Your First Tournament

The excitement of attending your first tournaments can cause forgetfulness, so make yourself a checklist to include everything you will need to compete. I went to the U.S. Open Skeet Championships very early in my competitive career—it was only about my third tournament—and I was very excited. I was so excited that I left my car at curbside when I checked my baggage at the airport. At about 30,000 feet and halfway across the country, I remembered the car, which by this time had been ticketed and towed away. Like I said, competition is exciting stuff. Make a list to keep the dumb moves to a minimum.

Scheduling Tournaments

At the beginning of each year it is good idea to make a schedule for the coming season. There are several good reasons for this. If you know when you will be attending major shoots, you can plan practice sessions to allow you to peak at the big tournaments. In between the big tournaments, you may want to schedule a few small ones to log some competitive experience. Or, if you are like me and do not have unlimited funds to spend on attending tournaments, you can plan your schedule around available funds.

Just having a schedule of the tournaments in which you plan to compete has a positive effect on how serious you are about practice. If you are planing to attend the Grand American in August, it isn't hard to begin serious preparations in late spring.

Until jogging and road races got so popular, the Grand American Trap shoot was the largest participant sporting event in the country.

As soon as the schedule is completed, make your room reservations, travel arrangements, and deposits to enter any big shoots you plan to attend. The big ones usually fill up fast. I guarantee you you won't get in the U.S. Open two weeks prior to the tournament.

Serious practice should begin to taper off a few days before the tournament. Light workouts are okay, but avoid shooting so much that you wind up burned out before the shoot ever starts.

I was lucky to have a good shooting instructor by the name of Dan Mitchell early in my career. Dan has coached many rookie All-American skeet shooters and gives extra attention to those students who take the game seriously. I remember he rounded up several of us who were attending our first World Shoot in San Antonio and took us to a movie the night before the tournament started. He said he didn't want us sitting in our rooms worrying about the next day or shooting targets in our minds. Of the four rookie shooters he had that year, two were selected to the Rookie All-American Team!

It is a good policy to arrive a day before a major tournament starts and shoot a few practice rounds just to become familiar with the club and shooting conditions. This is particularly important for sporting clays competitors. You need to know where the sun will be in the sky on the various fields. It can be disastrous to approach your last field of the day and discover that some of the targets you have to shoot are passing directly in front of a late-afternoon sun!

Just before turning in on the night before a tournament, I check all my guns and gear. Do I have the correct chokes in my gun? If I am shooting skeet, I make sure I have the right tubes in my gun for the first event of the day. It's embarrassing to arrive a

It's a good idea to arrive at least twenty minutes before your squad is scheduled to shoot and watch the targets, to make sure all your equipment is in order, and to allow your eyes to adjust to any changes needed in your shooting glasses. *Photo:* Jennifer Maier

little late and discover you have your .410 tubes in your gun and are supposed to be shooting 28 gauge!

Clean your glasses, and do all those little chores that can be done to avoid being rushed the next day. If for some reason you are running a little late and are forced to handle a lot of petty details just before you shoot, your anxiety level will undoubtedly go up.

On days when I am shooting in a tournament, I like to wake up a little early and lie in bed thinking positively about the day ahead. I visualize myself breaking targets and feeling good.

After I eat breakfast, I get to the club early. This gives me a chance to visit with friends from other parts of the country and let the jitters settle just a bit. It is also a good idea to arrive at your assigned field well before you are scheduled to shoot. Have your shooting glasses on so your eyes can adapt to whichever lens you have selected to wear. This adjustment takes about twenty minutes for most folks. Observe the targets. Are they affected by wind? Does the background make the targets hard to see?

Dealing With Distractions and Adverse Conditions

You should be thankful for rain, wind, cold, heat, and other foul weather. Poor shooting conditions are a blessing because they eliminate a good portion of your competition while helping you shoot a good score. Those folks who get all bent out of shape over the weather or some other distraction seem to think the rain is only falling on them or the wind is only blowing the targets around when they are shooting. I tell my students the wind is blowing everyone's targets. If your focus is on the wind or rain, that is probably all you will hit! Focus on the targets, and forget about all other distractions.

This is easier to do than most new shooters realize. You can only focus on one thing at a time. Forget the weather, because you can't do anything about it. Focus on breaking targets one at a time. You can do something about that. The first step in eliminating distractions is to make the decision to not let distractions bother you. This will get easier to do the more you work at it.

So much for the mental aspects of dealing with adverse conditions.

You might not be able to change the weather, but you probably can reduce its negative effects on you and your shooting. Now, let's deal with some of the physical aspects of shooting under adverse conditions, weather and otherwise.

Never cancel a practice session because it is windy, cold, hot, or raining. If there is lightning during a storm, the tournament will probably be canceled. If you have scheduled a practice and the weather becomes a bit inclement, go ahead on schedule. Practicing in bad weather is the only way to learn how to shoot in wind and rain. If you have practiced in bad weather you won't be so intimidated when the weather takes a turn for the worse in a big tournament. Just practicing in bad weather will give you a big edge on those fair-weather shooters who spend rainy afternoons on the couch. I have had competitive shooters call me when a front was approaching and ask for lessons during the bad weather.

Tape this on your bathroom mirror, on the dash of your car, on your computer, or refrigerator door, "Just remember that right now, someone, somewhere, is practicing and when you compete against him, he will beat you!" As Bobby Knight says, "The will to prepare to win is more important than the will to win."

Another key for dealing with adverse conditions is to dress properly. If you are shooting in a major tournament, arrive a day early. Go shoot a few practice rounds to get accustomed to the fields, backgrounds, and climate. I once attended a big sporting clays tournament in a Northern state and arrived a day early for a few practice rounds. In addition to the practice I was a major blood donor to some tiny winged varmint the locals called "no see'ums." The next day I was liberally doused with bug repellent. Those who arrived the day of the shoot were definitely distracted by these little vampires.

If you attend a shoot in a warm climate, you need to consider sunscreen, a hat with a brim, cool loose-fitting clothing, plus an abundant supply of Gatorade! I attended a World Skeet Shoot in San Antonio, Texas, in July and after every round I went to my shell bag for another box of shells and generous helpings of Gatorade. Stay away from carbonated drinks, caffeine, and alcoholic beverages when shooting in hot weather. The consumption of alcoholic beverages should always be postponed until the

When you go to your first major tournament, you might be intimidated by the huge numbers of competitors and all the "big guns" you have been reading about in the shooting magazines. Try to focus on each individual target, not on who might beat you. You can't shoot the other competitors; you can only shoot targets, one at a time. *Photo:* Jennifer Maier

guns are put away. If you don't have something like Gatorade, water is the next best choice.

The old outdoorsman's admonition to dress in layers certainly applies to clay target shooters. As the day warms up, layers can be removed to stay comfortable. If you are only wearing one heavy coat, then you may be reduced to only two choices as the day warms up—too hot or too cold. A thick, bulky jacket can also affect your gun fit and cause a negative result in your score.

Dealing With Pressure

If you are a new shooter, there will probably be a major distraction at your first mega-tournament that you never anticipated.

The big tournaments attract the big guns! I cannot remember

a single occasion where one of the "big names" in competitive shooting was anything but nice to me. But don't worry about who is shooting in the tournament. Many new shooters are so worried about who they are shooting against that they forget to focus on what counts. Targets are all that is going in the score book, so keep your priorities in order. You can't shoot your fellow competitors, only targets. If you work hard enough and long enough, you may someday end up in your very first shoot-off with one or two of the "legends." You have the advantage! They are the ones with the big reputations at stake, while you are a newcomer who most people will not remember the next week if you lose. But if you win, everyone will remember the greenhorn who bested "Mr. Big."

Just remember, Chapter 12, Verse 6 of the Gospel according to St. Jerry: "The only pressure in competitive shooting is what you bring with you!" With practice you will be able to take those competition jitters and turn them into feelings of positive expectations. It takes time and effort but it can be done.

Tip: Problem Targets

Many "problem targets" are not target problems but mental problems. We all struggle with a certain percentage of targets that account for a disproportionate number of our misses. For the trap shooter it may be a hard right crosser on post 5. For the skeet shooter it may be high 2. For the sporting clays shooter it may be springing teal. The first step in dealing with a problem target is to reclassify it. Stop thinking of it as a target that you have trouble with and start thinking of it as one you will learn to break. You have now transformed a "problem" to a positive goal.

Dreading a specific target and constantly thinking about how often you miss it will cause you to miss it even more often. Many shooters actually practice missing targets by visualizing themselves missing them. If you constantly replay your mental VCR

Positive attitude is important not only in competition but also in practice. Practice should be conducted with the same mental posture as competition. Be positive and upbeat. Winners expect to do well and win—losers get what they expect. *Photo:* **Jennifer Maier**

with an image of missing a target, you are using a powerful and effective visualization technique to program yourself to miss.

There are frequent references to "positive thinking," visualization, winning attitude, and what many competitors call "mind set." The first step to replacing negative visualization with the positive visualization used by the champion shooters is to learn the correct technique for breaking the target. Understand what I am saying here: I mean you must learn the correct technique and know the method for a specific target before you can break it consistently. Once you have learned the correct foot position, gun hold point, target break point, and, if you are using a sustained lead, what the correct lead is; once you have done your homework on the technical aspects of mastering a specific shot, you can use positive visualization of yourself breaking the target.

Once a technical problem has been identified, a portion of your practice session should be devoted to correcting errors in technique. As you begin to focus practice sessions on a "problem target," you will begin to transfer those mental images of yourself

Serious competitors like NSCA All-American Vicki Ash spend several days a week working on fundamentals. Each practice session has specific goals and is not just a casual afternoon at the range burning shells.

Every trap shooter owes it to himself to attend the Grand American Trap Shoot in Vandalia, Ohio at least once. Before road racing got so popular, the Grand American was the largest participant sporting event in the world.

missing the target into the positive attitude of "I can break this sucker!" Knowing the correct technique and having a positive attitude are two separate components for success that feed off each other. The more you work on technique, the more positive your attitude will become. But the more positive you are about breaking targets, the better your technique will be.

Many frustrated shooters often spend copious amounts of practice time, shells, and money practicing poor technique and thinking, "I can't break this target!" They are merely reinforcing the problem and perpetuating failure. Identify technical errors and correct them. Combine this with the positive visualization of breaking your problem target and you won't have a problem target.

This business of always maintaining a positive attitude and visualizing yourself destroying targets is not easy to master. It takes a lot of mental effort. Missing is easier than hitting a target. Likewise, it is easier to dwell on missed targets than to discipline yourself to mentally focus on executing perfect technique and seeing the target break in your mind.

Winners expect to win, and losers get what they expect!

Appendix

Addresses of Shooting Organizations

American Trap

Amateur Trapshooting Association (ATA)
601 W. National Road
Vandalia, OH 45377
(513) 898-4638

American Skeet

National Skeet Shooting Association
PO Box 680007
San Antonio, TX 78268-0007
1-800-877-5338

International Trap and International Skeet

National Rifle Association (NRA)
1600 Rhode Island Avenue N.W.
Washington, D.C. 20036-3270
(202) 828-6064

U.S. Shooting Team
U.S. Olympic Training Center
1750 E. Boulder Street
Colorado Springs, CO 80909
(719) 578-4587

International Trap

Pacific International Trapshooting Association (PITA)
PO Box 847
Redmond, OR 97754
(503) 548-6621

Sporting Clays

National Sporting Clays Association (NSCA)
PO Box 680007
San Antonio, TX 78268-0007
1-800-877-5338

General Information On All Shooting Sports

National Shooting Sports Foundation
555 Danbury Road
Wilton, CT 06897-2217
(203) 762-1320

Shooting Instructors and Instruction

Some of the foregoing shooting associations certify shooting instructors. You many want to contact them for information or a list. You can also contact your local trap, skeet, or sporting clays facilities and inquire about schedules for clinics and lessons.

Gil Ash (Sporting Clays, Skeet, Wingshooting)
PO Box 686
Bellaire, TX 77407
(713) 469-0101

East West Outdoors (weeklong sporting clays instruction)
PO Box 2770
Avon, CO 81620
1-800-323-4386

Hunter's Ridge Hunt Club (sporting clays, wingshooting)
3921 Barber Road
Oxford, MI 48371
(313) 628-4868

Frank Little (trap)
15 Ashley Drive
Dillsburg, PA 17019
(717) 432-4129

Jerry Meyer (sporting clays, wingshooting, skeet, trap)
RT 1, Box 309
Talking Rock, GA 30175
(706) 276-3363

Hill N' Dale Club
3605 Poe Road
Medina, OH 44256
(206) 725-2097

Kaye Ohye Corporation (trap, international trap, skeet, sporting clays)
600 Holly Lane
North Brunswick, NJ 08902
1-800-523-6493

Orvis Shooting School (sporting clays, wingshooting)
Manchester, VT 05254
(802) 362-3622

Sandanona Shooting School (sporting clays, wingshooting)
PO Box 800
Millbrook, NY 12545

Ed Scherer (skeet, sporting clays)
W. 30059 Woodcrest Drive
Waukesha, WI 53188
(414) 968-4788

Selwood Hunting Preserve (sporting clays, wingshooting)
RT. 1 Box 230
Alpine, AL 35014
1-800-522-0403

Shoot-Fire Sporting Clays (sporting clays, wingshooting)
290 Koostra Road
Bowling Green, KY 42101
(502) 781-9545

Vail Rod & Gun (sporting clays)
PO Box 1848
Vail, CO 81658
(303) 476-2662

Sporting Clays Course Design

Jon Kruger
RR 1, Box 213
St. Ansgar, IA 50472
(515) 736-4893

Dan Schindler
1142 Draymore Ct.
Hummelstown, PA 17036
(717) 274-8676

Wolf Creek Gun Club (skeet, wingshooting, sporting clays, trap)
3070 Merk Road S.W.
Atlanta, GA 30349
(404) 346-8382